# ART DECO

# ART DECO

Grange
BOOKS

A QUANTUM BOOK

Published by Grange Books
an imprint of Grange Books Plc
The Grange
Kingsnorth Industrial Estate
Hoo, nr. Rochester
Kent ME3 9ND
www.grangebooks.co.uk

1-84013-459-3

QUMADSI

This book is Produced by
Quantum Publishing
6 Blundell Street
London N7 9BH

Printed in Singapore by
Star Standard Industries Pte Ltd

# CONTENTS

# THE
# ART DECO
## STYLE

Art Deco is today regarded as a highly fertile chapter in the history of the applied arts. There is continuing debate, however, on the exact definition of the term 'Art Deco' and the limits of the movement it encompasses. When the Art Deco revival first began, around thirty years ago, it was viewed as the very antithesis of Art Nouveau – indeed, the theory was that the new style was spawned in 1920 to eradicate its predecessor, which history had already judged a grave, but mercifully brief, transgression against good taste. Today this theory has been proved incorrect: Art Deco is not the opposite of Art Nouveau; it is in many aspects an extension of it, particularly with its pre-occupation with lavish ornamentation, fine materials and superlative craftsmanship. Nor did it, as was previously believed, take root abruptly in 1920 and flower for a brief ten years until eclipsed by the economic collapse of the 1930s.

Although World War I has generally been taken as the dividing line between the Art Nouveau and the Art Deco epochs, in fact the latter was conceived during the transitional pre-war years and, like its predecessor, it was an evolving style that neither began nor ended at any precise moment.

### WORLD WAR I

Many items that are now accepted as pure Art Deco – such as furniture and *objets d'art* by Emile-Jacques Ruhlmann, Paul Iribe, Clément Rousseau and Paul Follot – were designed before or during the outbreak of hostilities, and thus the movement cannot be rigidly defined within the decade 1920–30. Had it not been for the four-year hiatus created by World War I, in fact, the Art Deco style would probably have run its full and natural course by 1920.

It is hard to define the main characteristics

*Right: This petite commode by Paul Iribe, 1912, was one of the furnishings commissioned for the Jacques Doucet apartment.*

*Opposite page: An elevator door from the Chrysler Building, New York, 1928–30, created by William van Alen.*

of Art Deco, because the style drew on such a host of diverse and often conflicting influences. Many of these came from the avantgarde painting styles of the early years of the century, so that elements from Cubism, Russian Constructivism and Italian Futurism – abstraction, distortion and simplification – are all evident in the Art Deco decorative arts vernacular. But this was not all: examination of the style's standard repertoire of motifs, such as stylised flower clusters, young maidens, geometry and the ubiquitous *biche* (doe), reveals various influences from the world of high fashion, from Egyptology, the Orient, African tribalism and Diaghilev's Ballets Russes. From 1925, the growing impact of the machine can be discerned in repeating or overlapping images, or later, during the 1930s, by streamlined forms derived from the principles of aerodynamics. All this resulted in a highly complex amalgam of artistic influences, defying description by one single phrase, though the term 'Art Deco', derived from the Exposition des Arts Décoratifs et Industriels Modernes held in Paris in 1925, remains perhaps the most appropriate one.

### A MODERN STYLE

The Art Deco style followed on immediately from Art Nouveau at the end of the nineteenth century. The latter had mostly relied on floral motifs to pattern and ornament its buildings and other artefacts, whereas Art Deco was thoroughly modern in turning away from the winding, sinuous qualities of Art Nouveau, looking instead to those of abstract design and colour for colour's sake; and when turning to

*Left: 'L'Oceanie' ('Oceania'), one of a series of exotic place images on a 1921 calender designed by George Barbier.*

8

nature for inspiration, it preferred to portray animals, or the beauties of the female form. Where Art Nouveau had been heavy, complex and crowded, Art Deco was clean and pure. The lines in Art Deco did not swirl around like the centre of a whirlpool; if they curved, they were gradual and sweeping, following a fine arc; if they were straight, they were straight as a ruler. After Art Nouveau, with its intricate and elaborate floral patterns and intertwining vines, and Empire and Consulate furniture, the coming of Art Deco and the pure, no-nonsense simplicity of everyday objects must have filled their users with a sense of relief and clean, uncluttered well-being. If Art Deco design was bold, bright and innocent, the reality of the age was far more sinister, far less comfortable and secure. Art Deco could be light-hearted on one level and deadly serious and practical on another. As the style in a time of unprecedented change, it was fluid enough to reflect that change.

## THE ORIGINS OF ART DECO

The style evolved in France, notably in Paris, where it manifested itself emotionally, with exuberance, colour and playfulness. Elsewhere in Europe, and later in the USA, it was given a more intellectual interpretation based on theories of functionalism and economy, and this element of design is known today as Modernism, to distinguish it from the high-style French variant, which is sometimes called 'high Art Deco'. Both, however, are aspects of a twentieth-century preoccupation with contemporary sources and inspiration, unlike the revivalism of pre-war styles.

*Right: An English enamelled cigarette case dating from 1931, its design clearly influenced by the Ballets Russes.*

*Above: One of the premier ceramics designers in Art Deco France was René Buthaud, who created this stoneware vase after attending the 1931 Exposition Coloniale in Paris featuring African art.*

Just as the Art Deco style had replaced Art Nouveau in France, so did Art Deco in turn yield to Modernism during the mid-1920s, its demise in fact beginning at its very moment of triumph, the International Exposition. The movement's first tenet – that form must follow function – remained unchallenged by any later schools of design, but its second, relating to decoration and craftsmanship, proved its undoing. By 1926, the loosely knit band of French Modernists – Francis Jourdain, Pierre Chareau, Le Corbusier, Robert Mallet-Stevens and René Herbst – had become increasingly outspoken in its criticism of those Art Deco designers who catered to select clients by creating elaborately crafted *pièces uniques*, or limited editions.

**THE MACHINE AGE**

The Modernists argued that the new age required excellent design for everyone, and that quality and mass-production were not mutually exclusive. The future of the decorative arts, they believed, did not rest with the wealthy few and should not be formed by their aesthetic preferences alone; an object's greatest beauty lay in its perfect adaptation to its usage. Each age must create a decorative style in its own image to meet its specific needs, and during the late 1920s this aim was best realised by industry's newest means of production: the machine. Existing concepts of beauty, based on the artisan and his hand tools, thus needed to be redefined to meet the dictates of the new machine age.

**THE INFLUENCE OF MODERNISM**

Modernism made rapid progress during the late 1920s, although most designers took a stance less severe than the functionalism that was espoused by its most ardent adherents.

*Left: Pierre Chareau designed this library for the 1925 Paris Exposition. He was an architect/interior decorator and his love of fine woods is evident in this elegant room.*

*Below: An advertisement for a British lighting firm illustrating a moderne chandelier designed in concentric circles.*

*Right:* Group of Dancers, *an elegant* moderne *ivory and bronze scupture by Paul Philippe.*

*Below:* The Metal Lady, *1923, by Russian sculptor Alexander Archipenko, whose work was defined by its abstract Cubism*

As Paul Follot, a veteran designer, observed in 1928: 'We know that the "necessary" alone is not sufficient for man and that the superfluous is indispensable . . . or otherwise let us also suppress music, flowers, perfumes . . . and the smiles of ladies!' Follot's viewpoint was shared by most of his designer colleagues – even if logic called for the immediate elimination of all ornamentation, humankind was not psychologically prepared for such an abrupt dislocation in lifestyle. Most designers thus opted for a middle ground, creating machine-made items that retained an element of decoration – which, ironically, had often to be hand finished.

### EARLY FUNCTIONALISM

Outside France, functionalism had a longer history, having dominated much decorative-arts ideology since the end of the Victorian era. In Munich, the formation of the *Deutscher Werkbund* in 1907 carried forward the logic and geometry at the heart of the Vienna Seccesion and Glasgow movements some years earlier. In contrast to both the French Art Nouveau repertoire of flowers and maidens, and Germany's own lingering *Jugendstil*, the Werkbund placed emphasis on those functional designs that could be mass-produced. A reconciliation between art and industry, updated to accommodate the technological advances of the new century, was thus implemented, with ornament given only secondary status.

### THE BAUHAUS

These ideals were realised more fully with the formation of the Bauhaus in Germany, which in turn inspired the Modernist strain that took root in American decorative arts during the late 1920s. After World War I, many European and Scandinavian designers followed the German example by creating Bauhaus-inspired

*Left: The Hoover Factory in London, 1933, designed by Wallis, Gilbert and Partners, incorporates Egyptian and other favoured Art Deco motifs.*

*Above: This carpet,* Arc-en-Ciel (Rainbow), *was produced by Lucien-Boux, c.1926, to a geometrical design by the French architect and interior decorator Eric Bagge.*

*Right: The dramatically illuminated spire of the Chrysler Building, 1928–30, lights up the New York night sky.*

furnishings and objects. Indeed, examination of contemporary European art reviews shows that ornament was sparingly applied outside France and, although a certain amount was tolerated, the high-style embellishments of Paris between 1910 and 1925 were viewed as a Gallic eccentricity which should not be permitted outside French borders.

The high style's only real success abroad was in American architecture, where it was adopted to enhance America's new buildings, particularly skyscrapers and film palaces. The USA lacked a modern style of its own during the early 1920s, so its architects looked to Paris for inspiration and leadership in art as they always had in the past.

### ART DECO'S WIDE-RANGING INFLUENCE

The paintings and graphics of the inter-war years are difficult to place in an Art Deco context. Many brilliant artists whose work falls beyond the proper scope of this book, such as Léger, Matisse, Vlaminck and van Dongen, at times incorporated motifs in Art Deco style into their works on canvas and paper. Others, such as Rouault, Dérain, Marcoussis and Braque, utilised a similar range of identifiable Art Deco motifs only when venturing into the field of the applied arts to design textiles and rugs.

### ARTISTIC CROSS-FERTILISATION

The boundaries between those who qualify as Art Deco exponents and those who do not are therefore far from finite. Most artists used a range of avant-garde mannerisms to solve traditional problems of design and composition. Some of these – for example, abstraction by means of Cubism and elongation, or the Fauves' preoccupation with bright colours – were used by almost every Modernist artist.

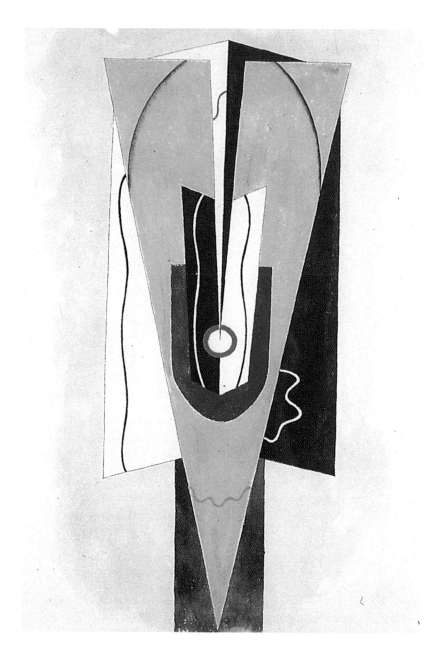

*Above: A carpet designed for Jacques Doucet by Louis Marcoussis, c.1926. The Polish-born Marcoussis was also a noted printmaker.*

*Left: Better known for his Cubist sculpture, the Hungarian-born Joseph Csaky created* Abstraction *in 1908.*

*Right: British ceramics designer Clarice Cliff created this charming musical duo as part of her* Age of Jazz *series of cut-out, painted figures.*

A study of painters who are considered today to fall within the Art Deco movement reveals certain common denominators by which an individual artist can be judged.

**DEFINING ART DECO ARTISTS**
Firstly, most Art Deco graphic artists were not innovative – they drew their inspiration from themes introduced by other Modernist artists, or schools of artists, often during the early years of the century, which they developed for their own purposes. Another criterion is that Art Deco graphics are decorative, designed to fit into the furniture ensembles of the era. Jean Dupas, for example, created paintings in a style which conformed to that of the furnishings in the room in which they would hang. They were, in the final analysis, decorative rather than artistic compositions. The same interpretation can be applied to the period's book illustrations and posters, many of which contained images found on contemporary ceramics, glassware and sculpture.

Yet it is precisely the mixing of all these influences that made Art Deco the style it is. In the hands of genius, the objects transcended their sources. In the hands of competent designers, or of plagiarists, they might become drab or garish, but they were, nevertheless, truly Art Deco.

# ART DECO
## PAINTING

*Preceding page: Aldo Severi's untitled oil painting illustrates Art Deco's preoccupation with the decorative elegance of the female and animal forms.*

*Right: Montmartre, 1925, an oil on board work by Jean Lambert-Rucki.*

*Below: This figure by Japanese-born artist Tsuguharu Foujita combines an Oriental technique with a Western subject.*

**P**ainting during the Art Deco period had tremendous variety: it could be decorative or avant-garde, sleekly streamlined or lushly ornamented, highly representational or markedly abstract. Not all works of art painted during the 1920s and 1930s can, of course, be termed Art Deco, since the term is generally applied to design and not to fine art. Indeed, there is really no such thing as specifically Art Deco painting. It is possible to talk of Cubism, Surrealism and Expressionism as coherent styles, but Art Deco painting never really existed in any convincing way. Strictly speaking, Art Deco derived its name from the Exposition des Arts Décoratifs et Industriels, which did not have a painting pavilion. Although the distance between the decorative arts and fine art as not as great as many people think, the best painting of the 1920s and 1930s certainly had little to do with the Art Deco style.

What does still exist, however, are examples of work by particular individuals that describe, or record in some way, the spirit of Art Deco, and some artists' works, whether because of their use of colour or geometric techniques, their stylisation or, more frequently, their inclusion in contemporary interior decoration or architecture, are nevertheless considered outstanding examples of the genre.

Art historians looking back at the art between the wars find examples of the best in the work of Picasso, Matisse and the Surrealists. There is really very little question that artists of the stature of Picasso, Mondrian, Kandinsky and others pushed forward the limits of painting, enriching the visual language beyond a stale academicism. Although these artists are now seen as the giants of twentieth-century art, it would be wrong to disregard the contributions of less well-known artists who communicated their message more readily, and also illustrated the taste of the age. Between the two extremes there is no contest on the grounds of quality, but minor art is often a more accurate indicator of public taste than the works of geniuses ahead of their time.

### ART AND GRAHIC DESIGN

Within the lexicon of 1920s and 1930s style, some of the most powerfully conveyed sets of images are held within the interlinked worlds of art and graphic design. Posters, illustrations and works of art have become interwoven with the style of these two decades, to the extent that one image is able to evoke a whole range of associations concerning the twenty years in question. It would be almost impossible to pin this phenomenon down to one set of reasons. Nevertheless, it is partially because of the extraordinary way in which, during this rich, highly creative period, various disciplines crossfertilised each other and grew together. Architects would design typefaces, painters would design houses, graphic artists would create costumes, poster designers would be influenced by architects, and so on. Therefore, while divisions between disciplines were still maintained, with artists essentially remaining artists and architects remaining architects, there was a distinct shift in the way in which practitioners within the various fields saw

*Left: This exotic urban landscape is a 1926 design for a backcloth by Russian artist Natalia Gontcharova for the Ballets Russes production danced to Stravinsky's* Oiseau de Feu *(Firebird).*

*Above: A Modernist students' apartmentt block designed by Walter Gropius, 1925, illustrates the Bauhaus style.*

themselves and applied their talents.

The prevalent atmosphere, that artists and designers were breaking new ground for a new age, meant that opportunities for experiments in different fields came into being more readily than had previously been known.

### THE SPIRIT OF THE AGE

Form and meaning within design in general shared motifs derived from a common interest in the redefinition of artistic and design parameters. It was as if a new language had been invented by an avant-garde which keyed into the modern obsessions with the machine and rationality and cut across the conventional boundaries between areas of design, art and theory. This was coupled with a feeling for the indeterminable, yet recurrent idea of the 'spirit of the age'.

There were certain events which facilitated the growth of this creative mélange. The setting up of the Bauhaus was one such event. The school was founded in 1919 in Weimar, Germany, now under the new regime of the socialist president Friedrich Ebert, and under the direction of Walter Gropius. It was not so much the thrust of the early Bauhaus teaching, with its attempt to wed art and craft, that makes it important in this context. More importantly, the school provided a focus for the artistic, creative and intellectual life of post-World War I Germany, which lasted for 14 brief years. At times the school acted as a clearing house for many of the foremost artists and designers in Europe. Indeed, several artists, painters, designers and architects considered prime movers in the world of design between the wars found their way to, and through, the Bauhaus. Paul Klee, Wassily Kandinsky, László Moholy-Nagy, Marcel Breuer and Mies van der Rohe are but a few.

*Right: A reproduction by Cassina of the original* Red and Blue Chair *of 1917 by de Stijl architect-craftsman Gerrit Rietveld.*

*Below:* Composition with Red, Yellow and Blue, *1937–42, by de Stijl artist Piet Mondrian.*

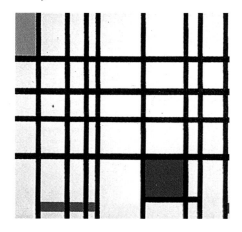

Definite links were forged between the Bauhaus in Germany and the de Stijl movement in The Netherlands, led by Theo van Doesburg and Piet Mondrian, and the *Vhutkemas* (art schools) in Russia, whose teachers included Kasimir Malevich, Vladimir Tatlin and El Lissitzky. This further added to the ferment of design theory and practice in Europe at this time. By the mid-1930s the *Vhutkemas*, the Bauhaus and the de Stijl movement had all met their demise. The rises of Stalin and Hitler put paid to the avant-garde tendencies of the institutions and movements in central and eastern Europe. These eventualities forced designers and artists to travel, and many set their sights on the New World,

making their way to England as a matter of course and leaving their marks, by way of influence and design and later by practice, in the United States.

### CROSSING THE DISCIPLINES

This cross-disciplinary influence, which is so characteristic of the inter-war years in Europe, can be seen in many instances. In 1920 Paris the Purist movement, led by Le Corbusier and Amadée Ozenfant, determined to produce art which employed the painting as a 'machine for the transmission of sentiment'. The magazine *L'Esprit Nouveau* was published at this time (from 1920 to 1925) and formed the basis of Le Corbusier's seminal 1923 book,

*Vers une Architecture* which contained the similar idea that the house 'is a machine for living'. Fernand Léger, too, professed to be influenced by the machine age and the subjects within his paintings took on the appearance of machined, cylindrical surfaces, far removed from artistic devices which had come before in his work.

### DE STIJL

In The Netherlands, the founders of the de Stijl movement also produced an eponymous journal to give vent to their own feelings about art, architecture and the world in general. The paintings of Piet Mondrian can be seen as the gradual rationalisation of perception and

representation into the horizontal, the vertical, primary colours and black, white and greys. Formally speaking, these ideas broadly tie in with the Modernist movement's aesthetic and can be found expressed to their fullest in Rietveld's 1925 Schröder House in Utrecht. Not an architect but a designer, Gerrit Rietveld built the house as a challenging exercise in three-dimensional planar composition, in much the same way that he had rendered his famous *Red and Blue Chair* in 1917, with colour picking out the structural detail.

### THE RUSSIAN STYLE

El Lissitzky, the Russian Constructivist artist who had been travelling in Europe during the 1920s, published an article on Rietveld upon his return to Russia in 1925, so aiding the spread and knowledge of European avant-garde ideas in art, architecture and design among the students and intelligentsia of yet another country. In Russia itself, the Constructivist movement had its own particular artistic language, adopted as the official revolutionary art. For those Europeans attuned to the thoughts behind Constructivism, it represented a reduction and rejection of traditional artistic representation and was wedded in purpose to social change and a strong belief in 'the machine'. Consequently, the power of industry – once in the hands of the workers – for bringing about change in the social order was the ultimate Utopian message. After 1921, when Constructivism was abandoned as the official revolutionary art form and the New Economic Policy was brought into action in the USSR, the artists behind the

*Left:* Tango, *casein on canvas by Erica Giovanna Klein. This images combines Cubist and Futurist influences.*

movement found that their ideas had no outlet. However, people like Moholy-Nagy, who had links with the Constructivists and who were later to become influential in imparting artistic theory and practice to their pupils at the Bauhaus, made sure that the principles of Constructivism were not allowed to die. Rather, they saw them instead subsumed into the general vocabulary of artistic usage.

### ANTI-ORNAMENTATION

Traces of the influence of the Constructivist idea are apparent in many images readily associated with European design during the 1920s. The fact that Constructivism, de Stijl and later Bauhaus ideas were expressed in a strongly geometric formal language only serves to heighten the sense that during the 1920s at least, the abandonment of unnecessary ornament in avant-garde, but obviously not *all* modern design, came to be seen as a powerful sign system. This in turn was seen to underline the existence of a common ground shared by forward-thinking designers working in all disciplines.

The formal language adopted by the avant-garde in Europe at this time cannot be viewed in isolation from the rest of the world of art. Indeed, the boundaries of what was possible and what was acceptable in terms of visual representation were opening up every day. The artistic language developed by Braque and Picasso had been realised relatively early in terms of the Art Deco period. Cubism, as a recognisable artistic style, existed by about 1915, but between the years 1920 and 1928

*Above:* La Naissance d'Aphrodite, *an oil on canvas painting by Paul Véra dating from 1925, depicted the birth of Venus in a Cubist manner.*

*Right:* Josephine Baker, *lacquer on wood,* c.*1926, by Jean Dunand.*

Picasso was still producing large Cubist still lifes like *Three Musicians* (1921) and *Three Dancers* (1925), which were, by then, very much a part of acknowledged art practice and therefore existed to be drawn from as part of a formal language.

The history books almost totally ignore the work of Tamara de Lempicka – surely the most representative of the period's portrait painters – the murals of Jean Dupas, the portraits of Kees van Dongen, or the later works of Raoul Dufy, reproducing instead the abstract innovations of Paul Klee, Pablo Picasso's classic nudes of immediately after World War I, or the rigidly thought-out and constructed canvases of Piet Mondrian. This actually misrepresents the prevailing taste of the period. The artists commanding the highest prices at auction in Paris between the wars were Maurice Utrillo and Maurice Vlaminck. In retrospect, we can see that the host of canvases they produced then were just watered-down versions of their early work, but that was what the public wanted. There is no use in being highbrow or snobbish about the decorative arts of the period – for even artists as great as Picasso were willing to turn their hands to stage design, pottery and furniture.

What is perhaps curious about the paintings that reflected the taste of the period most accurately was that they were almost always figurative, and in particular there are a great number of portraits that, even if we dismiss them as vulgar and modish, give a clear insight into the characters and tastes of their sitters. The large number of portraits or figure studies in the Art Deco style were really just illustrations of the period. Although there was generally little place for abstraction in Art Deco-style painting,, there were some exceptions to the rule.

### THE SIMULTANIST STYLE

Robert Delaunay and his wife Sonia had been deeply involved with the most advanced art in Paris since before World War I. Quickly adopting the lessons of Cubism from Picasso, Braque, Juan Gris and Fernand Léger, Robert Delaunay produced paintings of Paris – the Eiffel Tower, Saint-Severin Church – and such motifs of the modern world as the aeroplane and the motor car. By the time of the outbreak of the war, he had distilled his art into pure abstraction, where fields of intense colour collided with one another. Developing a style that was called 'Orphism', Robert Delaunay's work provided inspiration for Art Deco design. The sweeping, circular curves and fields of intense colour could be easily adapted to almost any other medium. It was his wife, however, who really developed and used the possibilities of the Simultanist style, as it was also known, to the full. Photos of Sonia Delaunay-Terk at the 1925 Exposition show her in Simultanist dress sitting on a motor car painted in the house colours. Her designs were all the rage, becoming *the* look for the sophisticated and avant-garde culture vulture. Bright and pleasing to the eye, her style brought a refreshing change after the heavy, exotic palette made popular by Bakst and Erté's costume designs for the Ballets Russes. The cut was also far more practical, severe and modern.

### FERNAND LÉGER

Another painter who is still regarded as important, and who could be said to reflect Art Deco preoccupations, was Fernand Léger.

*Above: The Russian-born Sonia Delaunay produced this watercolour, which she called* Simultané (Simultaneous). *The colourful fabric design is typical of the artist's bold, geometric output.*

*Left: Le Corbusier designed the Pavillon de L'Esprit Nouveau for the Paris Exposition of 1925. Its modernity caused a scandal among the organisers.*

*Right: An elaborate gouache in ink drawing by Jean Dupas, 1928.*

A friend and ally of Le Corbusier and Amadée Ozenfant, his pictures hung in the Pavillon de l'Esprit Nouveau at the 1925 Exposition. If Le Corbusier's architectural preferences were to provide houses that were machines for living in, Léger painted large murals and canvases that reflected the age's obsession with machinery. His canvases are peopled with robot-like figures painted in the brightest of colour combinations. What he aimed to do was to personalise the machine and employ it as subject matter, an attitude that ran throughout Art Deco in its more Modernist vein.

### MATISSE AND DUFY

The painters Henri Matisse and Raoul Dufy also contributed to the Art Deco influence. Matisse's interest in exotic subject matter, inspired by his visits to Morocco, reflected the contemporary French obsession with the colonies. Oriental art had been in vogue since the mid-nineteenth-century, but Matisse's exquisite sense of decoration reinstilled it with a vigorous, modern feel. Dufy, who had failed to win a commission for a large mural for the swimming-pool of the *Normandie*, produced painting after painting of the Côte d'Azur and Marseilles and its sailors at the same time as the south of France became the playground for the rich.

The many faceted nature of Jean Dupas' talent was also applied to painting. In Emile-Jacques Ruhlmann's pavilion, *Hotel d'un Collectionneur*, at the 1925 Exposition, Dupas displayed a large mural entitled *Les Perruches* (*'The Parakeets'*), a theme that was equally dear to Matisse. Dupas' many murals and screens for the *Normandie* and other private commissions, although executed in lacquer among other media, were in essence large paintings. Exotic and rich in subject matter, they were fine examples of the decorative tendencies of painting in the Art Deco style.

Tamara de Lempicka was probably the most typically 'Art Deco' of all the portrait painters, whose whirlwind social life and distinctive portraits reflected the glittering aspect of the Art Deco era and style. Born Tamara Gorska to a prosperous Polish family near Warsaw, she married a Russian, Thadeus Lempitzski (Lempicki), while in her teens. The couple arrived in Paris towards the end of World War I. Deserted by her husband during the 1920s, de Lempicka decided to support herself and her daughter Kisette by painting. She enrolled at the Académie Ransom, where she studied with Maurice Denis, a disciple of Cézanne,

*Below:* Dawn, *a gessoed-wood, 32-panel wall decoration for the Grand Salon of the ocean liner* Normandie *by Jean Dunand and Jean Dupas, c.1933-34.*

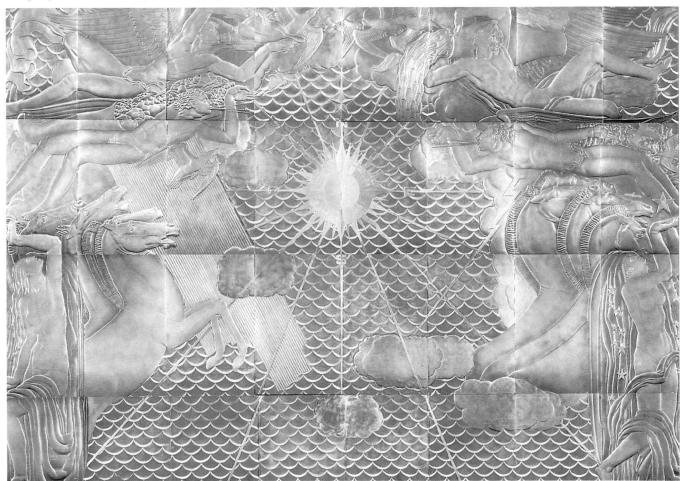

*Above:* Portrait of Arlette Boucard, *1928, by Tamara de Lempicka. It is a sensuous depiction of the daughter of a scientist who had invented the medicine Bacteol (written on the prow of a ship in the background).*

as well as André Lhote, the theoretician of Cubism. Thereafter she painted the portraits of other Eastern European refugees (mostly of royal lineage), famous writers, successful businessmen, fellow artists and her family. Her dramatic, vividly hued portraits were often sensuous and suggestive, sometimes surreal or frightening. Especially memorable are those with strong backgrounds, be they architectural or floral settings, or billowy folds of fabric, or a line of ships' prows.

### SENSUALITY AND SUGGESTION

In the view of some, de Lempicka's portraits of women, now in vogue again, are garishly hideous studies in eroticism. The Folies Bergères, Ziegfeld's Follies and Josephine Baker dancing in the nude are all highly suggestive and informative portraits of the risqué fast set that Nancy Cunard was part of. Semiclad nudes provoke the viewer with pointed breasts behind thin layers of diaphanous silk, or thin coverings of black Spanish lace. Like Foujita's sitters, or the hermaphrodite little girls in Balthus paintings, de Lempicka's sitters look at the spectator with a coy, languorous gaze. Between 1924 and 1939 she painted about a hundred portraits and nudes; these were dramatically composed works, usually boldly coloured (but sometimes black and white), highly stylised and charged with energy, sensuality and sophistication. Partly angled

Cubism, partly fashion illustration, they were positive expressions of the Art Deco style and should therefore have given her an accordingly classic reputation. Other painters of this sort of genre were Otto Dix and Christian Schad, who did for Berlin what de Lempicka had done for Paris, but rather better. Arguably, their work has been more enduring, too.

## MARIE LAURENÁIN

In sharp contrast to de Lempicka's handsome, somewhat aggressive works, were the ethereal paintings of Marie Laurenáin, which are often characterised as highly feminine because of their pastel hues, female subjects and innate 'prettiness'. They were nevertheless strong, distinctive images, and they appeared prominently within contemporary interiors, including those of her brother-in-law, André Groult. This versatile artist also designed rugs and carpets, as well as creating stage sets and costumes for the Ballets Russes' production of Francis Poulenc's *Les Biches*.

## RAPHAEL DELORME

Female figures dominated Art Deco canvases, and nowhere more boldly than in the paintings of Bordeaux-trained Raphael Delorme, whose bulky, muscular nudes were often situated in bizarre architectural settings, wearing incongruous headdresses or surrounded by fully dressed maidservants and mixed neo-classical and modernist images in a strange but appealing two-dimensional style. Indeed, an entire group of Bordeaux painters emerged during the Art Deco period, including not only Delorme, but also Jean Dupas, Robert Pougheon, André Lhote, René Buthaud and Jean Despujols. Although their monumental and allegorical paintings of women tended towards the neo-classical, they were

*Above:* Flamant Rose (Pink Flamingo)*, an oil on card painting by Raphael Delorme. The vase-bearing woman is seen amid a variety of Cubust motifs, with the title subject open winged behind her.*

*Above: A faience vase by the versatile artist René Buthard, 1925, featuring a monumental female figure typical of the Bordeaux painters' genre.*

*Above right: A* verre églomisé *panel by René Buthard, 1925 depicting a neo-classical, flower-draped nude.*

wholly of the period in terms of drawing and colours, as well as in such specific details as stylised flowers, make-up, hairstyles and costumes. Dupas, in particular, developed a highly distinctive and abstract style which captured precisely in its elongation and dehumanising expressions the general mood of the period.

Pougheon studied at the Ecole des Beaux-Arts in Bordeaux and then at that in Paris, where he developed an abstract style in which the subject's anatomy was given an angular muscularity of often heroic proportions. Some of his works are quintessentially Art Deco in their extreme stylisation, while others portray allegorical figures in naturalistic settings. Domergue painted portraits of Parisian socialites, theatre celebrities and nudes, in an engaging style in which certain facial features were exaggerated. Buthaud, like Dupas, switched media with great facility. His paintings, often rendered initially as cartoons for his stained-glass windows, or *verre églomisé* panels, incorporate all the softness and sensuality of his designs for ceramics. André Lhote was self-taught, and achieved landscapes, genre scenes and figural works which were somehow less caricatured and rather more starkly geometrical and spiritual than the works of the other painters.

### ANIMALIERS

Some French artists during the 1920s adopted a Modernist style in portraying animals. The premier *animalier* painters were Paul Jouve, Jacques Nam and André Margat, and they chose to treat their subjects in isolation, often silhouetted against a white background. Felines – leopards and panthers in particular – and snakes and elephants were popular, all painted in slightly abrupt or faceted brush strokes to reveal the beast or reptile's innate power and rhythm. Jouve was the most diverse, generating a large body of *animalier* etchings, drawings, watercolours, woodcuts and oils. He frequently worked with artists in other fields, such as Jean Dunand for murals on the ocean liner *L'Atlantique*, and with the bookbinder Georges Cretté to design plaques for his book covers.

One of the most popular Art Deco artists, especially in the United States, was the French-born Louis Icart, whose coloured lithographs, etchings and aquatints perfectly captured the image of the chic, attractive, sometimes slightly risqué woman of the 1930s, part Hollywood poster girl, part Parisian fashion plate. Typically, she reclined in a gossamer gown, her soft hair was usually Marcelled, her high-arched brows pencil thin, her eyes heavily shadowed and her lips perfectly reddened Cupid's bows. She was often smoking (a cigarette holder was almost obligatory) and was accompanied by an elegant dog, usually a greyhound, poodle or Borzoi.

*Left:* Fumée (Smoke), *a drypoint etching by Louis Icart, 1926. Icart specialised in painting women in erotic poses.*

*Right: A perspective of the Rockefeller Center in New York executed in pencil, paste and gouache on board by John Weinrich in c.1931.*

*Below:* Pearls, and Things and Palm Beach (The Breakers) *by Emil J Bisttram, a Hungarian emigré to the USA who worked in advertising and also painted* moderne *images.*

## THE AMERICAN STYLE

Austrian, Scandinavian and American painters also created works that can loosely be termed Art Deco, especially their stylised portraits of chic or androgynous women. The Paris-based American painter Romaine Brooks, for example, depicted Una, Lady Troubridge, in a dapper man's suit and with short hair, complete with monocle and a pair of dachshunds, while the Danish-born Gerda Wegener painted sensuous female nudes in erotic poses, but in distinctly modern settings. However, although such American artists as Stuart Davis, Georgia O'Keeffe, Rockwell Kent and Joseph Stella produced works in the machine-age idiom, celebrating industry, progress and big-city architecture, the vigorous Art Deco painting that thrived in France did not on the whole influence American artists, except perhaps in the occasional allegorical mural that embellished a movie-theatre lobby.

## ART OR KITSCH?

In conclusion, although it is interesting and anecdotal, no true Art Deco-style painting is ever great art, it is rather more an example of entertaining camp.

# ART DECO
# POSTER DESIGN

The basic stylisation – that is the geometricisation – of the Art Deco period lent itself well to graphics of all kinds, including poster, book and magazine illustrations, advertisements, packaging and the like, which, whether mass-produced giveaways or else limited-edition works of art, proliferated during the 1920s and 1930s. It is in poster design, where there is no question of high or low art, that an Art Deco style could truly be said to exist. During the 1920s, commercial art became a bona fide profession which, in turn, gave birth to the graphic artist. Graphic artists of the calibre of Rockwell Kent and Cassandre could employ all the devices of Art Deco design without needing to feel guilty. Their success relied directly upon their ability to reach the largest audience, to produce a popular image. Abstract art, which had taught so many designers the advantage of using clear form and strong, bold design, was not itself strengthened by Art Deco. It was, rather, watered down and made acceptable in its application to consumer items.

*Preceding page: A poster by Wilquin advertising* the Normandie *liner.*

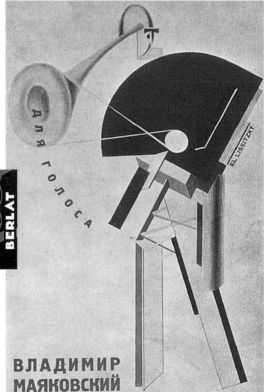

*Above: This French label for a chocolate bar is awash with Art Deco motifs and utilises a typical typeface.*

*Right:* For the Voice, *a strong Constructivist image by the Russian artist El Lissitzky.*

A particularly strong distillation of current visual languages between the wars can be found in the work of the poster designers in Europe, England and, to a lesser extent, the United States. The history of poster design really began during the late nineteenth century.

### THE HISTORY OF THE POSTER
Early posters had been used to illustrate the ambitions and aspirations of political parties or, on a more intimate scale, limited-edition prints by Rowlandson, Gillray and Honoré Daumier had provided a forum for the acid and biting criticism of the hypocrisies of the establishment. By the end of the nineteenth-century, artists like Steinlein, Henri de Toulouse-Lautrec, Aubrey Beardsley and Edward Penfield were producing works that truly understood the limitations and advantages of the poster medium. From them, other graphic artists learned the skills of successful poster design, as well as its role within twentieth-century society.

### TECHNICAL PROGRESS
Printing methods, especially colour reproduction processes, had vastly improved

*Left: A Blue Gillette advertisement dating from 1937. Strong sans-serif imagery had found its way into advertising by the 1930s.*

during the nineteenth and early twentieth centuries, as had the overall quality of the finished product, encouraging top-ranking artists and illustrators to accept commissions. Graphics had become bolder, broader, more geometric, less ornamented and, perhaps most importantly, highly legible. The first of the century's sans-serif typefaces, 'Railway', was designed in 1918 by Edward Johnston for the London Underground system.

### NEW TYPEFACES

The Bauhaus typographer Herbert Bayer's 'Universal' typeface, introduced in 1925, was void not only of serifs and other decorative elements, but even of capital letters. Even the Cyrillic alphabet took on strongly angular lines during the 1920s, in graphics by, among others, Vladimir Tatlin, El Lissitzky and Natalia Goncharova. In 1920s' France, however, decorative touches were added to – rather than subtracted from – typefaces, a logical development considering the vogue for decoration in every other medium. This was manifested primarily in the juxtaposition of thick and thin elements within a single letter, or in decorative shading that entirely eliminated a part of a letter. M F Benton's *Parisian* (1928) is a good example of thick-thin characters, while Cassandre's *Bifur* (1929) consisted of letters that were nearly unrecognisable, except for their grey areas.

Until the advent of commercial radio after World War II, the poster campaign was by far the most effective way of reaching a mass audience and informing it of the product on offer. Of course, the realisation that, in a world

*Right: A poster for Imperial Airways, 1930s. Travel advertisements celebrated the beauty of the machine as much as the exotic destinations promoted.*

dominated by the poster, new posters had to be simple and powerful just to get their message across must have had an impact on the way in which the poster was conceived. That there was a large and varied 'scrapbook' of visual ideas available to the poster artists to draw upon, in the guise of avant-garde art and architecture, was only to their benefit.

Posters had to be cheap to mass-produce, striking in design and arresting enough to catch the viewers' attention for long enough to tempt them to read the accompanying text. This latter attribute was not even essential, as the poster could work on the same level as a medieval stained-glass window, educating and informing an illiterate audience and

suggesting to them what they might like to acquire. Although the message was more mundane and down to earth than that of the medieval craftsmen, the result in terms of beauty was not necessarily less. The best and most memorable posters were equal to, if not better than, much so-called 'fine art', and this was especially the case with Art Deco.

## THE GROWTH OF ADVERTISING

The Art Deco poster was the first full-blown example of a sophisticated understanding of the advantages and idiosyncrasies of the world of advertising. This was hardly surprising, as the growth of the advertising industry and the medium of poster design were inseparable. Art Deco, the style of the consumer age, was applied with great success to the promotion of all the new consumer items, including the gramophone (phonograph), radio set, motor car (automobile), aeroplane, ocean-going liner, cosmetics, household appliances and, of course, the Hollywood movies.

## DYNAMIC SUBJECTS

The motifs of many of the vividly coloured posters and graphics of the period were characterised by sheer energy and exuberance, in part the result of the new obsession with speed and travel that accompanied the fancy motor cars, fast trains and elegant ocean liners which were so much an expression of the 1920s and 1930s. The one lasting theme and motif that ran throughout Art Deco posters and illustrations was that of the modish, self-possessed and highly energetic woman. She would be the role model that any woman bent on self-improvement would have to emulate. Ever changing, she inspired people to part with their money in order to keep up with her. Unlike the idealised nudes and nymphs that peopled Art Deco sculptures, the women in posters were modern in every sense of the word. The sketches of Ernest Deutsch Dryden are a superb contemporary record. Women in the latest fashions stand with their companions around a Bugatti motor car ready to step in and set off – to where? Deauville, Cannes, Long Island or a weekend party at a country house?

*Above: A poster-type caricature of the French performer Maurice Chevalier, who first achieved fame in Paris revues of the 1920s. Note the sans-serif typeface.*

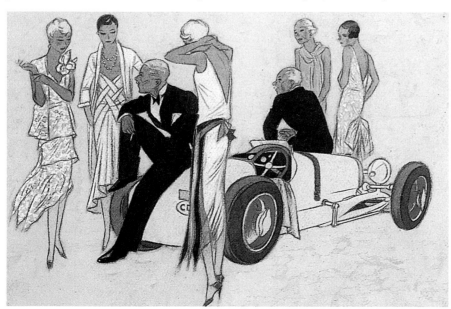

*Left: Ernest Deutsch Dryden's pencil and gouache image of fashionably dressed people grouped round a Bugatti motor car.*

*Right: A M Cassandre's lithographic poster for the Alliance Graphique, dated 1935, promotes Dubonnet.*

*Below: The dramatic foreshortened design on the Celtique cigarette poster is the creation of A M Cassandre, 1924.*

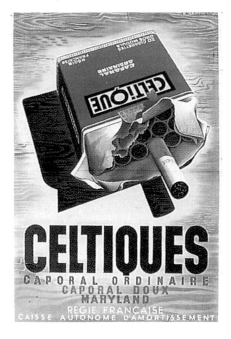

Dramatic, colourful and enduring, Art Deco posters can be divided broadly into two categories: theatrical and commercial (including travel and special events such as sports meetings, concerts and art exhibitions). In Germany and Italy, the poster also became a dynamic (and extremely effective) propaganda tool for the Fascist regimes.

### A M CASSANDRE
Perhaps the greatest poster designer and typographer of Art Deco Paris was the Russian-born Adolphe Jean-Marie Mouron, better known by his pseudonym Cassandre. Certainly his work is regarded as being among the most evocative of the period, and it was arguably the most successful of his time. His distinctive graphic style – bright colours combined with subtle shading, bold lettering often juxtaposed with wispy characters, and strong and angular, flat images – won him numerous awards. Between 1923 and 1936 Cassandre used the poster as no one had before him. In his hands it represented an interface between the visual languages of the avant-garde and the ordinary public. The adept use of the pictogram, bold typeface and skilful lithography meant that a combination of the elements of Constructivism, Cubism and Modernist typeface design came together as a commercial tool and, many critics would say, a work of art.

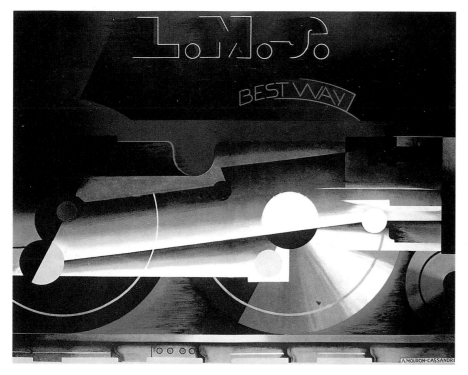

## IMAGES OF TRAVEL

Cassandre was a self-confessed lover of architecture and hated 'deforming details'; it is no accident, therefore, that some of his most enduring images were produced to advertise railways and shipping lines. After all, these posters were to represent the very machines which inspired the architects, which in turn inspired the artist. Thus, his poster *Nord Express* (1927), in which a streamlined, angled locomotive puffs decoratively, and his most famous single work, the fiercely frontal view of the ship for his poster for the liner *Normandie* (1935), represent the opposite ends of Cassandre at his most precise. In *Normandie*, the prow of the ship pushes forward out of the picture, as the majestic giant dwarfs the small tug beneath it. The stark outlines of the design and the stylised realism of the picture suggest to the viewer the qualities that the *Normandie* certainly had: including strength and elegance. In such posters, his work most reflected and utilised the current modern machine aesthetic-inspired visual language. As representations of distilled 1920s and 1930s' style, they are hard to better.

## PAUL COLIN

Cassandre was not the only poster artist operating in Paris. Indeed, when this period in Paris is discussed, it is often in terms of the three 'C's: Cassandre, Colin and Carlu. Paul

Colin – whose often light-hearted illustrative style, although neither as austere nor as classy as Cassandre's, was equally effective – designed posters to advertise the visiting jazz luminaries at the Folies Bergère and other venues. Originally the poster artist and stage designer for the Théâtre des Champs-Elysées, he is perhaps most famous for his poster for 'La Revue Nègre' of 1925, the show which introduced Josephine Baker to Paris, in which a saucy Josephine Baker is memorably depicted with two black jazz musicians.

### 'THE JAZZ STYLE'
It is with posters like these that the Art Deco style came closest to gaining the name 'the jazz style'. Deriving loosely from Cubist painting with its disjointed sense of perspective, the colours were jazzed up, as unlikely combinations of electric blue were juxtaposed with reds and livid greens. The overall effect was initially jarring, but then resolved itself into an energetic and fully comprehensible pictorial logic. Colin's posters were in a style rather reminiscent of that of Marc Chagall, the artist who had been the art commissar of Vitebsk in Russia in 1919. Colin took a similar route, moving away from figurative representation to a more geometric style which was inspired by Constructivism, consisting of overlapping planar surfaces. This style is particularly in evidence in his work for the Wiener and Docet Piano Company. Before this, Colin designed a series of posters to advertise Josephine Baker's recordings, as well as depicting Miss Baker in several paintings. He also designed stunning posters advertising not only other

*Left: A 1925 poster by Paul Colin advertising the 'Black Revue'. This is perhaps his most famous work.*

*Above: Robert Bonfils' poster advertising the 1925 Paris Exposition Internationale des Arts Décoratifs et Industriels Modernes.*

*Left: This poster advertises the Chicago World's Fair of 1933. Note the patriotic colouring, the prominence of the androgynous winged head and the fading image of the Native American.*

XXIᵉᵐᵉ SALON DES ARTISTES
DECORATEURS

GRAND
PALAIS

côte
Champs
Elysées

METRO
CHAMPS
ELYSEES

de mai
a juillet
1931

*Above: René Buthard's 1931 poster for the Société des Artistes Décorateurs.*

performers, but cigarettes and other products, most of which featured human figures, sometimes highly stylised, sometimes lovingly caricatured in recognisable detail.

### JEAN CARLU

The third 'C', Jean Carlu, can also be seen as a representative of the verve, vitality and adaptability of creative people in Paris at this time, untrammelled by the idea that one discipline was enough. Carlu trained as an architect but, after losing his right arm in an accident, gave up architecture and moved on to poster design. His output was of a similar standard to Cassandre and Colin's, but gravitated towards less glamourous goods, *Mon Savon* soap of 1927 and consequent advertisements for toothpaste being among his most successful executions.

Another artist operating in Paris at the same time, designing both posters and packaging, was Pierre Fix Masseau, whose Cassandresque style in the French Railway's *Exactitude* poster of 1932 served to underline the effectiveness and popularity of this style. Charles Gesmar, who is best remembered for his posters of the Casino de Paris performer Mistinguett, designed in a curvilinear and ornate style, *à la 1900*. He usually employed stark lettering, but occasionally became rather fanciful, with his letters resembling those of Jean-Gabriel Domergue on his posters for the dancers Maarcya and Gunsett.

Three memorable posters were created for the 1925 Paris Exposition by Charles Loupot, Robert Bonfils and Girard. Loupot's designs cleverly juxtaposed industry and decoration, depicting a massive factory with wisps of black smoke cutting across clouds shaped like stylised flowers. Bonfils' image was totally decorative, featuring a stylised Greek maiden carrying a basket of flowers, accompanied by a dark, leaping deer.

## RENÉ VINCENT

Another notable poster designer, René Vincent, forsook his architectural studies at the Ecole des Beaux-Arts in Paris for a career in the graphic arts and, to a lesser degree, ceramics. An illustrator for *La Vie Parisienne, The Saturday Evening Post* and *L'Illustration*, Vincent also designed posters for the giant Parisian department store Au Bon Marché. His compositions often featured fashionable demoiselles playing golf, or bearing parasols, done in a crisp illustrative style that was heightened by contrasting blocked colours.

## OCCASIONAL POSTER DESIGNERS

Many other French graphic artists provided the world of poster art with intermittent works. Jean Dupas, for example, turned his hand to a series of delightful advertisements for Saks Fifth Avenue, Arnold Constable and others, with a facility that shows his great versatility. René Buthaud transposed the maidens on his stoneware vessels onto paper, some to herald the annual Paris salons. The identity of the prolific artist Orsi, whose name appears on more than a thousand posters, including images of Josephine Baker at the Théâtre de L'Etoile, remains an enigma. From the world of fashion, Gorges Lepape and Natalia Goncharova created posters in a predictably colourful and theatrical style which depicted Paris as the pleasure capital of the world.

In Britain, the United States and Germany, most poster designs were pared down and geometric, using the bold, rectilinear typefaces

*Right: Joost Schmidt's poster for the Bauhaus 'Art and Technology' show, 1923.*

that were fast becoming the norm. Among the primary exponents of the art of the poster in Britain was Edward McKnight Kauffer, an expatriate American who settled in London in 1914 (and returned to the USA in 1940). His poster design in *Flight* (1916) is different from these transportation images: a highly stylised representation of a flock of birds, it was inspired by a Japanese print as well as marked by the influence of the Vorticist movement, which flared briefly during World War I in London. It appeared in *Colour* magazine, which devoted one page per month to a poster design. This design was later taken up to advertise a national newspaper in 1919. Kauffer thought of himself as a painter until 1921, the year in which his work as a poster designer took off and he was able to

*Right: A colourful and decidedly* moderne *poster for London Transport by C Paine, 1918.*

*Far right: This stunning poster for Fritz Lang's* Metropolis, *1926, betrays a German Expressionist influence in its graphics and the inspiration of New York in the cityscape.*

consolidate his position. Prior to this, Kauffer had worked for Frank Pick, head of publicity on the Underground Electric Railway Company of London, producing posters of Watford, Reigate and other rural places accessible by means of London Transport. These posters depended on a relatively simple, but stylised, representation of a landscape to suggest the idea of day-tripping to nearby ideal spot. While his London Transport posters tended to be quite Cubist and abstract, those of other designers were more colourful and representational, but always with easy-to-read typefaces. The French artist Jean Dupas, for example, designed a poster for London Transport showing a scene of elegantly dressed ladies in Hyde Park.

## KAUFFER'S SIGNIFICANCE

By the mid-1920s Kauffer had consolidated

his position in Britain as a leading poster designer; indeed, in 1925 there was a retrospective exhibition of his work featuring 56 of his designs, of which among perhaps the most famous today is his poster for Fritz Lang's masterpiece *Metropolis* and also for Shell Petroleum. After this point, Kauffer's work expanded to meet the influence coming from the continent, taking on board the motifs which are today so readily associated with this era. Kauffer also pioneered photomontage techniques, collaborating on several occasions with the celebrated photographer Man Ray. He further illustrated the tendency for designers to work in more than one medium by his designs for rugs (his wife, Marion Dorn, was a celebrated rug designer) and his collaboration with architect Wells Coates on the wall mural at Embassy Court, Coates' seaside block of flats in Brighton (1935).

## BELGIAN AND DUTCH DESIGNERS

In Belgium, the Swiss-born Léo Marfurt formed a fifty-year-old association with the tobacco company van der Elst, for which he designed advertisements, packaging and posters. In 1927 he formed his own studio, Les Créations Publicitaires, where he produced two world-class masterpieces of travel-poster art: the *Flying Scotsman* (1928) and *Ostende-Douvres* (around 1928). The former emerged as one of the most recognisable, enduring and popular images of the inter-war years. René Magritte, a magazine and advertising illustrator before he turned to Surrealism, also created some vibrant Art Deco poster images during the mid-1920s, while two other Low Country artists, Willem Frederik ten Brock and Kees van der Laan, produced posters for Dutch shipping lines.

## SWISS AND GERMAN DESIGNERS

In Switzerland, Otto Baumberger, Herbert Matter and Otto Morach designed for the fashionable men's clothing store, PKZ, as did the German Ludwig Hohlwein. Baumberger, trained as a lithographer and posterist in Munich, London and Paris, worked principally in Zurich, where he helped to establish the Swiss School of Graphic Design. Matter is known principally for his pioneership of the photomontage technique in travel posters such as *Winterferien* (1934) and *All Roads Lead To Switzerland* (1935). Ludwig Hohlwein was Germany's most popular and prolific poster artist. His preference for virile, masculine images with which to advertise coffee, cigarettes and beer later won him many commissions for Nazi propaganda posters.

*Left: An advertisement for the PKZ men's clothing-store chain, 1923.*

*Above: A Lucien Bernhard poster, 1929 .*

*Left: A detail of the publicity poster for the movie,* The Shape of Things to Come, *1936.*

### THE PARISIAN INFLUENCE

Hohlwein's real gift lay in his use of colour in unexpected combinations. Other German posterists, such as Walter Schackenberg and Josef Fennacker, embraced a softer, French-inspired style in their designs for theatre and ballet performances.

The Hungarian Marcel Vertès established himself immediately after World War I as a leading poster artist in Vienna. He moved in 1925 to Paris where, apart from the publication of two volumes of lithographs, *Maisons* and *Dancing*, and occasional work for Elsa Schiaparelli, he lapsed into obscurity. His Viennese posters, however, were colourful and distinctly Parisian in their light mood.

Brilliant interpretations of the Art Deco poster were produced in other countries, but with less frequency, by Marcello Dudovich and Marcello Nizzoli in Italy; Maciej Nowichi and Stanislawa Sandecka in Poland; and Kauffer, Alexander Alexeieff, J S Anderson and Greiwirth in Britain.

In some ways the poster, and design in general, across the Atlantic was to be deeply affected by the arrival of artistic and design talent from Europe. As the Nazis became more and more powerful, Europe became an increasingly difficult place in which to exist, and many artists emigrated.

### DESIGN IN THE UNITED STATES

The list of names that finally found their way to the United States reads like a design hall of fame for Europe. The Austrian-born Lucien Bernhard, for example, had studied at the Munich Academy, from which he emerged as a versatile artist-architect, designing buildings, furnishings and graphic works. In 1923 he emigrated to the United States, where in 1929 he co-founded the Contempora Group in New York. His poster style appears laboured and undirected, but he was invariably treated with respect by contemporary critics.

### LESTER BEALL

As far as home-grown American talent was concerned, the field was dominated by Lester Beall, a self-taught graphic artist whose clever use of photomontage and Modernist typefaces helped to promote, among other

He stands alone as the greatest entertainer of modern times! No one on earth can make you laugh as heartily or touch your heart as deeply...the whole world laughs, cries and thrills to his priceless genius!

Charlie Chaplin in MODERN TIMES

Written, Directed and Produced by Charles Chaplin

Released thru United Artists

things, the Works Progress Administration (WPA) which was part of President Roosevelt's popular 'New Deal' from 1935.

By this time Beall was surrounded by European talent: Cassandre, Mondrian, Carlu, the artists Max Ernst and Marcel Duchamp, Bauhaus teachers Gropius, Herbert Bayer, Breuer and Moholy-Nagy, and photographers Man Ray and Cartier-Bresson.

### EUROPEANS IN THE UNITED STATES
Clearly, at this time in the United States the thrust for innovative graphic design was coming from Europe. Even famous American graphic icons, such as Raymond Loewy's bold design for the Lucky Strike cigarette pack in 1940, owe a great deal to the influence of Bauhaus-inspired sans-serif graphics. And the official posters for the 1939 New York World's Fair, depicting the quintessentially American image of the Trylon and Perisphere, came from the pen and airbrush of an expatriate Austrian, Joseph Binder. He, too, drew inspiration from the popular 'scrapbook' of Modernist and avant-garde images which formed the basis of 1920s and 1930s' style in the graphic arts. The work of Vladimir V Brobritsky, another highly talented immigrant, likewise captured the vibrant, alluring mood of inter-war Paris.

*Above: A poster produced to publicise Charlie Chaplin's movie* Modern Times, *1936.*

# ART DECO
# BOOKBINDING
# AND ILLUSTRATION

*Right: A four-panel screen by Jean Dunand, featuring a trio of monkeys amid tropical vegetation. Dunand used similar motifs and techniques in bookbinding.*

*Below: Pierre Bonoit's* Mademoiselle de la Ferté, *1926, binder Pierre Legrain, illustrations by Yves Alix.*

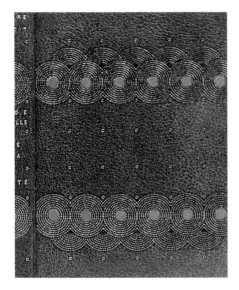

*Preceding page: A rare and lavishly bound copy of Charles L Philippe's book* Bubu de Montparnasse, *designed by Paul Bonet.*

**O**ne of the most exciting areas of graphic Art Deco design was the book jacket, as well as the binding that encased the book. Indeed, the craft of bookbinding underwent a renaissance after World War I, although most observers were unaware that it had in earlier times attained a high degree of artisanship.

By long tradition, books in France had been published with flimsy paper covers, making them acceptable to the serious collectors who employed bookbinders to design and create covers for their favourite volumes. This system prevailed right up to the earliest years of the twentieth century. The binding's function was to preserve the text, and it was not considered as a means of artistic expression until the emergence of the Art Deco movement. At that point, however, the principles of artistic excellence together with excellence in craftsmanship caused a radical change. During the 1920s Paris was filled with small presses, but as well as these there was still a strong tradition of wealthy people, like Huysmans' hero des Esseintes in *Against Nature*, who had their favourite books specially bound.

## BOOKBINDING

Although book design may seem in some ways superfluous to the actual purpose of a book, no one who has held a fine-tooled, Morocco-leather binding in the hand, and turned the pages of handmade paper, can deny the sensual delights of sight, touch and smell and the pleasures of good design and craftsmanship that such a book can give. A particularly fine example was the collaboration on the book *Bubu du Montparnasse* in 1929 by Charles I Phillipe. The binding, designed by Paul Bonet, was accompanied by illustrations by the artist Dunoyer de Segonzac.

## PIERRE LEGRAIN

Pierre Legrain, a noted furniture designer must be credited with revolutionising the art. In 1912, when Jacques Doucet disposed of his collection of antique furniture at auction, he presented his correspondingly important library of eighteenth-century books to the city of Paris, retaining only his collection of works by contemporary authors. The young Legrain, who had been more or less unemployed since his former employer Paul Iribe set sail for the United States in 1914, was retained to design the bindings in a modern style. Without prior experience, and largely self-taught, Legrain undertook the task in the *atelier* of the binder

*Below: An opulent 1936 leather binding by J K van West covers Maurice Barrè's book* La Mort de Venise.

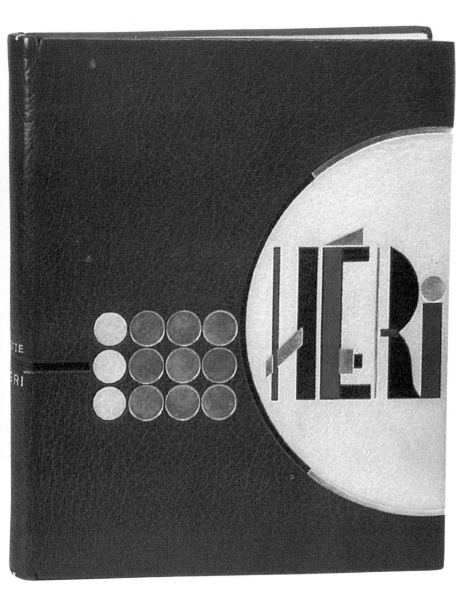

*Above: A stamped and foiled Morocco-leather book binding for Colette's* Chéri *designed by Rose Adler in 1925.*

*Above right: François Coppée's* Le Passant, *bound by Georges Adenis.*

René Kieffer. Doucet was at once impressed and commissioned more bindings. In a two-year period Legrain designed some 365 bindings for Doucet, all of which were executed by professional binders. By the early 1920s, Legrain's abilities had drawn the attention of other collectors, such as Baron Robert de Rothschild, Henri de Monbrison and Baron Gourgaud, all of whom became regular and valuable clients. Legrain introduced an unusual and endearing selling ploy, donating to the patron the tools used on each binding.

### THE AVANT-GARDE IN BOOKBINDING
Legrain's ignorance of traditional binding techniques served him well, for it allowed him to make free use of his creativity and to introduce materials not used before. From the start, his designs were avant-garde, in keeping with the revolution in design taking place

throughout the decorative arts in Paris. In place of the lightly ornamented floral bindings of the pre-war years, he introduced geometrical patterns in the same precious materials being employed at the time by Modernist *ébénistes* such as Emile-Jacques Ruhlmann, Clément Rousseau and Adolphe Chanaux.

Indeed, some of the top names in French design applied their talents to book covers and sometimes used the same opulent materials as in their furniture and other designs.

## BINDING MATERIALS

By the 1920s, bookbinding had become an extension of the Art Deco cabinet-making craft, as exotic veneers and skins were borrowed in search of a means to modernise the age-old craft. Most Art Deco bookbinders incorporated bright colours, geometric elements and sumptuous materials into their work. Hides such as snakeskin, *galuchat* (sharkskin) or vellum were interchanged with binding's traditional Moroccan leather. Decorative accents were provided in innumerable ways. For instance, the binding could be inlaid with a mosaic of coloured leather sections, or with gold, silver, platinum or palladium fillets, or it could be gilt-tooled, blind-stamped or painted.

## DECORATIVE PLAQUES

Further embellishment was provided by the application of decorative plaques in sculptured or veneered wood, lacquered silver or gold, enameled porcelein, bas-relief bronze or carved ivory. The encrustation of mother of pearl, tortoiseshell or semi-precious stones provided further aesthetic possibilities. Exotic works were covered with Japanese prints or silk-mounted on cardboard. A matching slipcase completed the package for unique works. Although most of the premier Art Deco

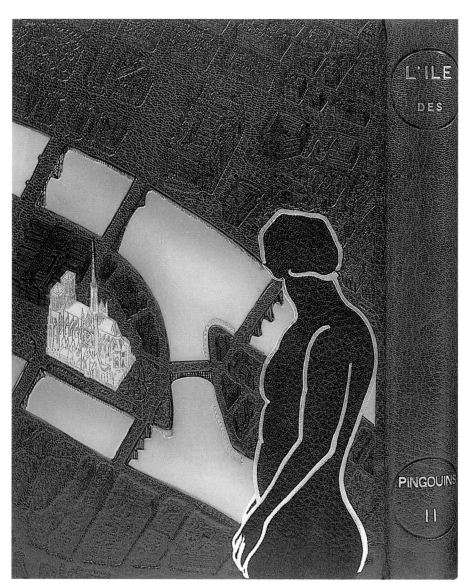

*Above:* L'Ile des Pingouins, *by Anatole France, 1926, bound by Henri Creuzevault.*

*Right: A menu designed by the versatile François-Louis Schmied in 1926 for his friend Jean Dunand.*

*Below:* Histoire Charmante de l'Adolescent Sucré. *The medallion was designed by François-Louis Schmied and executed by Jean Dunand; the binding is by Léon Gruel.*

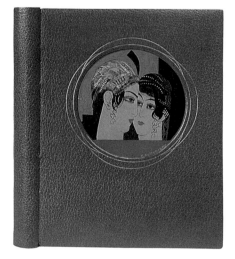

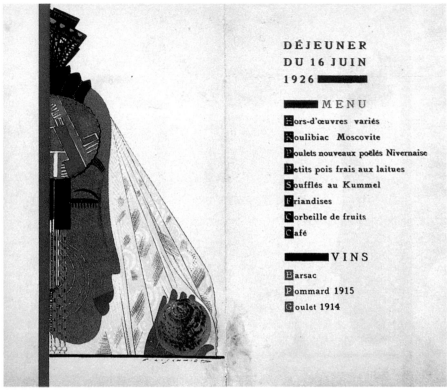

DÉJEUNER
DU 16 JUIN
1926

MENU

Hors-d'œuvres variés
Koulibiac Moscovite
Poulets nouveaux poêlés Nivernaise
Petits pois frais aux laitues
Soufflés au Kummel
Friandises
Corbeille de fruits
Café

VINS

Barsac
Pommard 1915
Goulet 1914

bookbindings included no letters on their covers, some incorporated the titles effectively, using gilt *moderne* letters to complement the prevailing geometric motifs.

### MOTIFS AND SUBJECTS
The 1920s' binder drew mostly on the same repertoire of motifs used in other media. Combinations of lines, dots, overlapping circles and centripetal or radiating bands were used to create symmetrical or asymmetrical compositions. The influence of the machine and new technology became increasingly felt towards 1930, particularly by Paul Bonet, who

emerged as Legrain's successor. The preferred motifs of the Paris salon during the early 1920s (such as the stylised floral bouquet or gazelle,) quickly yielded to a fiercely geometric vocabulary found especially in such works as Creuzevault's *La Seine de Bercy au Point-du-Jour*, Legrain's *Les Chansons des Bilitis*, Kieffer's *Trois Eglises* and Bonet's *Les Poilus*.

As well as Legrain, Paris was home to a host of premier binders who worked in the Modernist idiom, including Georges Cretté (the successor to Marius Michel), René Kieffer, Jean Dunand, Paul Bonet, François-Louis Schmied, Louis Creuzevault, Georges Canape

*Far left: Maurice de Noisay's* Tableau des Courses, *1921, a book bound by Charles Benoit and illustrated by J L Boussingault.*

*Left:* La Creation, *elegantly bound by François-Louis Schmied (who also provided the illustrations) in collaboration with Conin et Cie.*

and Robert Bonfils. Foremost among these was another Doucet protégée, Rose Adler, whose bindings for Doucet were even more exotic than Legrain's, and were sometimes encrusted with precious stones. Her maroon Morocco-leather binding for Colette's *Chéri* (1925) is stylish, with 12 metallic circles at the left giving way to a huge hemisphere at the right, which is actually the letter 'C' enclosing the last four letters of the title.

## ROBERT BONFILS

Legrain rarely designed figural bindings, but others, notably Bonfils, did – usually sharp-angled or modishly decorative silhouettes, seldom full-colour figures. Bonfils was himself also an executor of bindings, working with André Jeanne, a professional binder who produced designs for Rose Adler and for

*Left: J C Mardrus'* Ruth et Booz, *1930, bound and illustrated by François-Louis Schmied; lacquered panel designed by Jean Dunand.*

55

such other gifted practitioners as Paul Bonet and the father-and-son team of Louis and Henri Creuzevault. Louis Creuzevault created abstract or floral patterns, as well as covers with three-dimensional applications of differently coloured leathers. In 1930 he produced a binding for Georges Duhamel's *Scènes de la vie future* that was distinctly *moderne*.

### ARTISTIC COLLABORATIONS

Many of these binders collaborated on commissions with artist-designers, and even with other binders. Schmied, in particular, was extremely versatile, participating in commissions as a binder, artist or artisan with Cretté and Canape. The *animalier* artist Paul Jouves and the sculptor Guino contributed designs for ivory and bronze panels. Jean Dunand was likewise very active, creating lacquered and *coquille d'oeuf* plaques, and even wooden ones inlaid with detailed marquetry designs, for Schmied and other binders. His plaques were sometimes designed by Schmied, and included colourful landscapes, stylised floral motifs, abstract patterns and exotic figures and animals. One handsome example was a striking roundel illustrating a panther and a young man for Rudyard Kipling's *Jungle Book*, or *Le Livre de la Jungle*.

### FRANÇOIS-LOUIS SCHMIED

François-Louis Schmied, a man of many talents, not only designed covers but illustrated books; designed both them and their typefaces; created their lettering; made wood engravings of illustrations for them; and even printed them on his own presses. His bindings ranged from

*Left: An English book cover created by American-born designer Edward McKnight Kauffer, who also designed carpets.*

subdued monochromatic enlivened only by gilt lettering to opulently multi-coloured, often set with lacquer panels, usually executed either by Dunand or else by the Cubist-influenced designer Jean Goulden. A lovely Schmied binding for Paul Fort's *Les Ballades françaises* featured a green and silvered-metal plaque by Dunand showing stylised birds on a background of dots in a rainbow pattern.

### PAUL BONET

Paul Bonet, a fashion designer turned bookbinder, was imaginative and innovative, using metallic bindings; cut-out bindings that revealed a design on the endpapers; and other related but varying designs and lettering on the spines of works of more than one volume, such as on Marcel Proust's classic *A la Recherche du temps perdu*.

Some binders also incorporated photographic elements in their covers, among them Laure Albin Guillot, who specialised in microphotography, enlarging tiny biological specimens – such as plankton, – to produce unusual, pseudo-abstract designs. Many of her other bindings included human images, such as an erotic, back-posed nude on Pierre Loüy's *Les Chansons de Bilitis*.

### LESSER BOOKBINDERS

Less well known were the works of Paul Gruel, André Bruel, Jean Lambert, Alfred Latour, Jeanne Langrand, Yseux, Louise Germain and Germaine Schroeder, whose creations in many instances matched those of their more celebrated colleagues. The new enthusiasm for bookbinding also drew in graphic artists, for example,

*Right: A French poster utilising a similar typeface and geometric design to the book covers of the period.*

Maurice Denis, George Barbier, Georges Lepape and Raphael Drouart. The artist-turned-decorator André Mare incorporated a pair of love birds, in engraved and tinted parchment, for his cover design for *Amour*, commissioned by Baron Robert de Rothschild.

In other Western countries, the finest bookbinders adhered largely to traditional materials, methods and designs.

**BRITAIN AND THE UNITED STATES**
However, mass-produced, printed covers in Germany, Britain, the United States and elsewhere also depicted Art Deco figures and motifs. The stylised lettering which came to be associated with 1920s' Paris was also often seen. A 1932 English-language edition of Bruno Bürgel's *Oola-Boola's Wonder Book* displays such lettering – bold, in several sizes and decorated in blind-stamping with simple vertical and horizontal bands.

In the United States, the Greek-born John Vassos and Ruth Vassos designed and produced bindings of note, often for their own, coloured-cloth-on-board books, which included *Contempo* (1928), *Ultimo* (1930) and *Phobia* (1931). These catchy, contemporary titles appeared in thick, bold lettering on grounds highlighted by equally bold geometric designs. Vassos was also known for his industrial designs. The American-born Edward McKnight Kauffer, then working in Britain, was responsible for the book jacket for H G Wells' *The Shape of Things to Come* (1935).

The book and fashion-magazine illustrators of the 1910 to 1914 period anticipated the later Art Deco graphic style. Inspired primarily by the 1909 arrival in Paris of the Ballets Russes and Léon Bakst's vivid stage and costume

*Left: This lovely illustration by the British graphic artist and illustrator John Austen adorned the frontispiece of a 1928 limited-edition of 500 copies of* Manon Lescaut.

*Far left: The delicate ornament and costume of Asia, as reinterpreted in Art Deco style by George Barbier, 1920.*

ANTINÉA

Manteau du soir, de Paul Poiret

designs, French commercial artists followed suit, introducing an orgy of colours and medley of Persian, Oriental and Russian influences into their designs for book illustrations, fashion plates and theatre sets. Couturiers such as Paul Poiret provided additional opportunities in the same style for such employees as Erté and Paul Iribe, by publishing volumes of their newest fashions.

### FASHION ILLUSTRATORS

By the time of the outbreak of World War I, Bakst-inspired *pochoirs* and aquatints dominated the pages of Paris's foremost fashion magazines, *La Gazette du Bon Ton*, *L'Illustration* and *La Vie Parisienne*. The first mentioned in particular drew on the talents of a host of artists, including George Barbier, Edouard Garcia Benito, Georges Lepape, Robert Bonfils, Umberto Brunelleschi, Charles Martin, André Marty, Bernard Boutet de Monvel and Pierre Brissaud. These artists mixed eighteenth-century pierrots, columbines, powdered wigs and crinolines with women clad in the latest *haute-monde* creations. From 1920, the lightly sensual young woman of these transitional years was transformed into a chic *garçonne* (girl-boy), a wilful coquette who indulged in sport and cigarettes.

### ERTÉ

Of these illustrators, the Russian émigré Erté (born Romain de Tirtoff) gained lasting fame as a designer – first in Paris and later in the United States. Not only did he create minutely detailed fashion plates from 1913 until after World War II, but he was still working at the

*Left: A fashion plate created by Georges Lepape which appeared in* La Gazette du Bon Ton *in 1920.*

*Left: A highly stylised holiday greeting card dating from c.1925 signed by the artist Renbal.*

time of the Art Deco revival during the 1960s. Between 1924 and 1937 he was exclusively contracted to design covers and illustrations for *Harper's Bazaar*. Working in a manner closely allied to Parisian Art Deco, Erté did much to convey a fashionable European sophistication among other American magazines, a highly desirable ability when Europe was in vogue as *the* fashionable place. Erté also worked in other disciplines, thus continuing the penchant for the multimedia designer. Consequently, the success of his stage sets, fabric designs and graphics meant that he attained unparalleled status on two continents as a designer with his finger on the pulse of European-inspired *Art Moderne*.

### GERMAN ILLUSTRATORS

Elsewhere in Europe, response to the French Art Deco style was sporadic and mixed. In Germany, the fashion revue *Die Dame* followed the lead of its French counterparts, as did the German-born illustrator Baron Hans Henning Voigt, who worked under the pseudonym Alastair, creating haunting images that were inspired by Edgar Allan Poe. Alastair spent most of his career in England before moving to the United States.

### AMERICAN FASHION MAGAZINES

The French Art Deco graphic style reached the United States during the late 1920s, where it quickly evolved into a Modernist idiom in which the machine's influence was increasingly felt. Fashion magazines such as *Vogue* and *Vanity Fair*, *Harper's Bazaar* and *Woman's*

*Left: A 1939 watercolour of a stylish interior by André Edouard Marty, whose illustrations often appeared in the* Gazette du Bon Ton.

*Above: William Welsh's cover for the February 1931 issue of the American magazine,* Woman's Home Companion.

*Left: Erté's exotic costume design for the character of Assad in the ballet* Dance de Jouet *from* A Thousand and One Nights.

*Left: This 1920s' advertisement illustrates the Art Deco preference for sans-serif typefaces and geometric motifs.*

*Home Companion* included French-inspired stylisations in their advertisements. To impress their readers, editors invited such European illustrators as Erté, Benito and Lepape to contribute cover designs. Other periodicals, such as *The New Yorker* and *Fortune*, tended towards a more geometric and industrial style, especially for their covers.

### THE EUROPEAN INFLUENCE
Once settled in the United States, European designers found their voices in the pages of the fashion magazines. Notable among them was the Russian-born poster designer Alexey Brodovitch, who had been working in Paris but was the art director at *Harper's Bazaar* from 1934. He employed the likes of Salvador Dalí, Man Ray and Henri Cartier-Bresson to provide photographs and, with consummate skill, fundamentally altered the rules governing the way in which magazines were to look.

### AMERICAN MODERNISTS
Other noted Modernist designers working in the United States during the 1920s and 1930s included Joseph Binder and Vladimir V Bobritsky – both European expatriates – and the native-born William Welsh, John Held, Jr and George Bolin. During the 1920s, Rockwell Kent pursued a light Art Deco graphic style in his woodcuts for book illustrations, while John Vassos, the country's premier Modernist in book design, imparted a powerful linearism to his covers and illustrations.

# ART DECO FURNITURE AND METALWORK

# A TRANSITIONAL STYLE

*Above: a postcard advertising a Manhattan shop selling Art Deco designs.*

*Left: Emerson, the American firm, produced this radio in the 1930s. The red Bakelite body is typical of radios of the time.*

T**he term 'Art Deco' means different things to different people – but in a very specific way. To purists, for instance, it implies opulent Parisian furnishings. To students of Modernism, on the other hand, it suggests minimalism in design. To romantics the term recalls glittering Manhattan skyscrapers. And to aficionados of industrial art it evokes memories of Bakelite radios.**

The school of luxuriant French design which reached its peak at the 1925 Paris World's Fair – the Exposition Internationale des Arts Décoratifs et Industriels Modernes, whence the term Art Deco is derived – is generally considered pure, high-style Art Déco (with an accent on the 'e'). Over the years, however, the output of other schools and countries of the so-called 'machine age' has come to be covered by this catch-all term, which, incidentally, was not current during the period,

and did not begin to be used until the 1960s.

Thus, the parameters of Art Deco (usually without the accent), or *Le Style 25*, as others call it, have expanded to include a wide array of modern Western architecture, design, decoration, graphics, motifs, products and even fine art dating from approximately 1915 to 1940, with the 1939–40 World's Fair in New York acting as an endpoint of sorts. Some non-French Art Deco works relate directly to Parisian design – the furniture of the German

*Opposite page: William van Alen's Chrysler Building in New York is crowned by a nickel-chromed steel spire.*

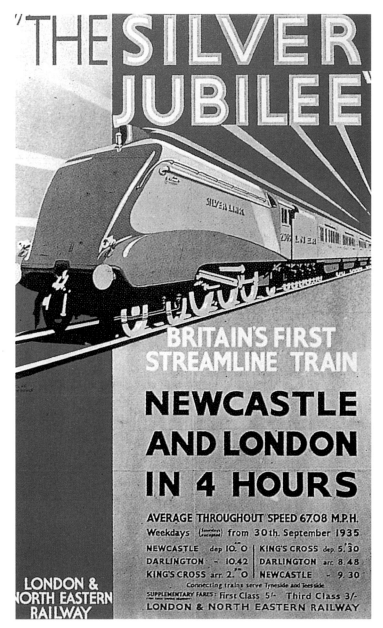

'THE SILVER JUBILEE'

SILVER LINK

LNER

BRITAIN'S FIRST
STREAMLINE TRAIN

NEWCASTLE
AND LONDON
IN 4 HOURS

AVERAGE THROUGHOUT SPEED 67.08 M.P.H.
Weekdays (Saturdays excepted) from 30th. September 1935
NEWCASTLE dep 10. 0 | KING'S CROSS dep. 5.30
DARLINGTON - 10.42 | DARLINGTON arr. 8.48
KING'S CROSS arr. 2. 0 | NEWCASTLE - 9.30
Connecting trains serve Tyneside and Teesside
SUPPLEMENTARY FARES First Class 5/- Third Class 3/-
LONDON & NORTH EASTERN RAILWAY

LONDON &
NORTH EASTERN
RAILWAY

Bruno Paul or the jewellery of the American firm Black, Starr & Frost, for instance. Many other designers throughout Europe and the USA paid vestigial homage to the French style, among them the creators of the spectacular American and English motion-picture palaces, the Russian-born Serge Chermayeff, and the British potter Clarice Cliff, with her jazzy, brightly hued ceramics. Still others, such as the Bauhaus school of the Scandinavian glassmakers, created their own distinctive and original styles, blazing new and seemingly antithetical trails to those being forged by most of the French.

### A MULTI-FACETED STYLE

So, far from being a school of design that is characterised only by geometric forms, or by lavishly decorated surfaces, stylised flowers, lithe female and animal figures, vivid colours and the like, as so many think of it, Art Deco is a multi-faceted style for all seasons, and for all tastes.

### THE SPARKS OF MODERNISM

The seeds of Art Deco were sown well before the 1925 Paris Exposition, indeed, as early as the last years of the nineteenth and the first years of the twentieth centuries, when Art Nouveau still reigned supreme. This nature-inspired, essentially curvilinear and asymmetrical style experienced its zenith at the 1900 Exposition Universelle, which also took place in Paris, but its decline began soon afterwards, hastened in part by the rise of industrialisation. Art Deco was modern because it used aspects of machine design as inspiration. It

*Left: a 1935 poster for the* Silver Jubilee, *touted as 'Britain's first streamline train'. The Art Deco period was the machine age.*

68

was even more modern because it accelerated the adoption of such new, materials as plastic, Bakelite and chrome.

The sparks of modernism were set off in Vienna, where the architect-designers Otto Wagner (1841-1918), Josef Hoffmann (1870-1956) and Koloman Moser (1868-1918) started a trend towards rectilinearity which was to be adopted, either consciously or not, at first by French and German and later by American designers. Some of the Austrians' furniture, glass and flatware designs, even those as dating from early as 1902, are quite modern looking. In the same way, the Glaswegian Charles Rennie Mackintosh (1868-1928), who was much admired by the Viennese, created furniture, interiors and buildings which reflected an understated, proto-modern sensibility with their light colours, subtle curves and stark lines. They were a world apart from the uninhibited, undulating designs of his French contemporaries. Two Mackintosh clocks, both dating from 1917, are modern, rectilinear and architectonic. They even make use of Erinoid, a synthetic made from resin or protein plastic.

*Below: a gilt and lacquered carved wood panel attributed to Paul Véra.*

*Right: Josef Hoffmann's masterpiece of 1905–11, the Palais Stoclet in Brussels, Belgium, demonstrates Hoffman's standing as a transitional figure between Art Nouveau and Art Deco.*

Even before Mackintosh, British designers created mass-produced pieces with startling, modern looks. The silver and electroplated tableware of one of the most accomplished, Christopher Dresser (1834-1904), whose pitchers, candlesticks, tureens and tea services were designed during the 1880s ,is now displayed in such esteemed and decidedly contemporary collections as that of the Museum of Modern Art in New York.

### THE ARTS AND CRAFTS MOVEMENT

The English Arts and Crafts movement, although very much grounded in medievalist principles, practices and institutions such as the guild, could also be said to have exerted some influence on Art Deco, albeit in a surprisingly roundabout way. The lead came chiefly from its early American exponents, who then inspired later designers in the United States. Frank Lloyd Wright (1867-1959), for instance, some of whose achievements late in life were quite streamlined and Bauhaus-like, had adhered to Arts and Crafts-type aesthetic for most of his career, even when producing mass-made furniture.

### EXOTIC INFLUENCES

But the French designers whose works have come to exemplify Art Deco – Emile-Jacques Ruhlmann, Jean Dunand, Armand-Albert Rateau, Süe et Mare, René Lalique *et al* – were influenced less by their immediate European predecessors than by earlier periods, and even by far-off, exotic places, *if* they can be said to have been dependent on outside factors at all.

### PRIMITIVE AND ORIENTAL ART

To trace the sources of Art Deco is indeed a difficult exercise. Since the style had so many often unrelated and even contradictory manifestations, its inspiration can only have been both manifold and diverse. Best-known among the influences are African tribal art, Central American (Aztec and Mayan) architecture and pharaonic Egyptian art, this last due in large ·part to the discovery of Tutankhamen's tomb in 1922. Influential as well were the bold designs and bright colours of the Ballets

Russes, the glazes and lacquerwork of the Far East and the imagery and metalwork of classical Greece and Rome. French furniture forms of the Louis XV and Louis XVI periods also contributed, and even contemporaneous fine arts such as Fauvism, Constructionism and Cubism played a part, mostly in terms of colours and shapes, especially as applied to textiles.

## Functionalism

There were, in addition, the truly modern visionaries, such as Le Corbusier (1887-1965) and his associate Charlotte Perriand (b. 1903), whose functional furniture, or 'equipment', as they termed it, was also sharply reductionist (that is, simplified to its utmost), and is still very influential today. Interestingly, Le Corbusier's stark, all-white Pavillon de l'Esprit Nouveau, at the 1925 Paris Fair, was in marked contrast to the ostentatious exhibits of Süe et Mare's Compagnie des Arts Français, Lalique,

Ruhlmann and others, yet its statement was as strongly modern – in retrospect even more so – than theirs.

## Industrial design

The exponents of the streamlined school of the Art Deco period were primarily from the United States, where industrial designers such as Raymond Loewy, Walter Dorwin Teague and Walter von Nessen helped to define modern culture with their tableware, hardware, household appliances, automobiles and aircraft. Though blatantly antithetical to the Gallic school, the work of these talented Americans shaped the future in a positive, exciting way that was not at all grounded in a romantic and ornamented past.

## The cross-fertilization of styles

Other Americans, however, borrowed colourful, decorative elements from their French counterparts and included them in their

*Above: a figure of a Japanese fan-dancer from the Preiss-Kassler workshop, c.1929. Oriental art inspired Art Deco.*

*Left: a macassar ebony, marquetry, giltwood and marble commode made by the Compagnie des Arts Français.*

modern architectural creations. Structures like the Chrysler and Chanin buildings in Manhattan were latter-day temples of a kind, but devoted to industry and business rather than to any spiritual deity. Architects throughout the United States working in their own Art Deco vein created factories, apartment complexes, hotels, and, of course, film theatres. Indeed, although the Parisian architect-designers were responsible for buildings as well as for interiors and furnishings, it was their New World counterparts who really excelled in these large-scale works.

### INTERDISCIPLINARY INFLUENCES

The Art Deco period is renowned for its contributions to other disciplines, as well as to architecture, furniture and industrial design. These include textiles and carpets, fashion, bookbinding, graphics (embracing posters, typography and advertising) and two entirely new fields in their time: lighting and cinema. Glass, ceramics, silver and other metalwork, jewellery, painting and sculpture were also treated in entirely Art Deco ways.

Indeed, one of the most important aspects of the 1925 Exposition was the impact of pavilions on the four major Paris department stores. Each of these stores had realised that quality and price could be supplemented by good design, and each had its own design studios. The recognition that a retail outlet could profit by employing designers provided a boost to the whole industry. Even specialist producers of glass, porcelain and ironwork at the luxury end of the market had to maintain exceptionally high standards in order to compete.

### ART DECO REASSESSED

What of the Art Deco style today? The great *objets*, of course, produced at the height of

*Above: this Mornington & Weston baby grand piano and stool, c.1930, incorporates architectonic elements into its design.*

*Left: a detail of William van Alen's Chrysler Building, New York City, 1930.*

*Below: a promotional brochure advertising the Chanin Building in Manhattan, designed by Sloan & Robertson, 1929.*

chanin

building

another chanin achievement—at new york's front door

the period's creativity, are prized possessions in museums and private collections, and many of the finest buildings are today being conscientiously conserved by caring enthusiasts and civic officials. Even mass-produced baubles and *bric-à-brac* are now being sought after and saved.

## ART DECO'S POPULARITY TODAY

Books on the subject have proliferated since the early 1970s, covering scholarly aspects of furnishings and architecture, and making the designs of the day available to graphic artists. Dealers specialising in Art Deco – from kitsch ornaments to objects of museum quality – can be found both in big cities and country towns, and antiques fairs and auctions devoted

entirely to the period have sprung up as well. Tours of Art Deco architecture are now offered in Miami Beach, New York and Tulsa, Oklahoma, and other places will no doubt soon follow suit.

## Contemporary reproductions

Some of the world's top designers and craftsmen are now producing furniture and architecture with Art Deco-style embellishments, and many great pieces of the 1920s have been revived by excellent contemporary reproductions. The Italian firm Cassina, for instance, offers copies of Rietveld's famous *Red and Blue Chair*. The Parisian interior designer Andrée Putman's Ecart International has brought out some of Eileen Gray's rugs and her *Transat* armchair, as well as Robert Mallet-Stevens' dining-room chairs and a Jean-Michel Frank and Chanaux sofa. Chairs by Le Corbusier, Marcel Breuer and Mies van der Rohe have become design classics which continue to be produced, and even Parker has recreated a classic 1927 fountain pen, featuring it in an advertisement along with a Cassandre poster, an Eileen Gray table and a Bauhaus lamp, all again also in production.

## Art Deco revived

The Cristal Lalique glass firm still makes several pieces created by René Lalique during the 1920s and 1930s, and Clarice Cliff's colourful *Bizarre* ware is being manufactured again and sold in the china departments of exclusive stores. Art Deco typefaces, graphics and colour combinations often appear in

*Left: South Beach, Miami, boasts many fine examples of Art Deco architecture.*

*Left: an elaborate wall sconce designed by the great Parisian ironworker Edgar Brandt.*

*Left: architect and interior designer Pierre Chareau designed this library for the 1925 Paris Exposition, where it was featured in the Ambassade Française.*

*Above: a collection of the highly decorated pottery of Clarice Cliff. The pieces' simple forms are jazzed up by means of daring colour combinations.*

advertisements, and many stores and restaurants give prominence to Art-Deco-style fittings, furniture and menu designs. Contemporary films are frequently set in the 1920s and 1930s, with stunning period interiors and costumes, and interest in the original films themselves has intensified, with video cassettes readily available and revivals often taking place in 1930s' picture palaces.

Despite the implicit diversity of the style's theme, interest in Art Deco is not waning. The subjects and the artefacts attributed to it are likely to remain a source of fascination for decades to come. The following chapters will celebrate the Art Deco spirit as it was applied to furniture and metalwork, and will thereby show why it was that this inter-war period was among one of the richest and most exciting in design history.

# FRENCH
# ART DECO
# FURNITURE

The period from 1905 to 1910 was a transitional one, during which the style now known as Art Deco began to evolve in Paris. Its major proponents seem to have had two primary objectives concerning design. The first was the desire to remove all traces of foreign influence in order to return to a purely French mode. As André Véra wrote: 'Thus for furniture we will ... continue the French tradition, ensuring that the new style will be a continuation of the last international style we have, that is the Louis-Philippe style'.

*Previous page: a rounded display cabinet created by Paul Follot in dark wood and ivory with a carved floral motif.*

Consequently, French taste in furniture was expressed by a return to eighteenth- and early-nineteenth-century style – Louis XV, Louis XVI, Consulate, Empire and Directoire – adapted to contemporary taste. The second of the objectives in forming a new style was to abolish the curve, which had been used as a primary mode of expression in Art Nouveau furniture. Disciplined, stylised bouquets replaced the whiplash stems of Art Nouveau.

New organisations were established in France during the first decade of the twentieth century to enable designers of decorative objects to exhibit their work at regular intervals. The most important of these was the Société des Artistes Décorateurs, formed in 1901. The founding members of the Société des Artistes Décorateurs included prominent designers and architects from the Art Nouveau era, including Eugène Grasset, Hector Guimard and Eugène Gaillard, in addition to individuals who emerged as leaders of the Art Deco movement: Emile Decoeur, Francis Jourdain, Maurice Dufràne, Paul Follot and Pierre Chareau.

*Right: A highly stylised two-panel screen of lacquered wood created by Léon Jallot in 1928.*

## FURNITURE DESIGN IN TRANSITION

Other major designers during these transitional years were Léon Jallot, Paul Iribe (who was to spend a considerable period in the United States), Louis Majorelle, Mathieu Gallerey, Pierre and Tony Selmersheim, Charles Plumet, Théodore Lambert and Henri Bellery-Desfontaines. Their work can be considered as a somewhat modified and simplified version of Art Nouveau, in which increasingly angular compositions were lightly adorned with carved motifs. A bookcase exhibited by Jallot at the 1908 salon provides a typical example of the changing style, its simple form incorporating a curvilinear apron.

## THE EMERGENCE OF ART DECO

Further ornamentation was provided by an upper row of panels naturalistically carved in a restrained Belle Epoque manner. However, the veneers were rich and varied, in anticipation of the coming 1920s' style. In 1912, Follot presented a suite of dining-room furniture at the Salon d'Automne in which the chairs and commode were enhanced with pierced baskets of flowers that appear today as high Art Deco – that is, from the mid-1920s rather than the pre-war years. Ruhlmann incorporated the same stylised motif, with modifications, in his celebrated *encoignure* of 1916, indicating that the Art Deco style in furniture would have

*Above left: a group of two rosewood* bergère *armchairs and two matching* boudoir *chairs in the style of Paul Follet.*

*Left: this petite commode by Paul Iribe dates to 1912, and was one of the pieces commissioned by Jacques Doucet.*

reached maturity by 1920 if not for the unavoidable hiatus caused by World War I.

Two important events occurred during these pre-war years to influence the evolution of the Art Deco style in furniture. In 1909 the Ballets Russes, directed by Diaghilev, opened in Paris. The sets, designed by Léon Bakst, were brilliantly coloured, with bold patterns. These sets, coupled with the savage colours of the Fauves, who exhibited at the 1905 Salon d'Automne, helped interior designers move away from the restrained palettes of the previous era, and to incorporate an unprecedented brilliance in their schemes. Radiant reds and greens were used for cushions, and bold abstract and figural patterns for upholstery, draperies and wallpapers.

## THE SALON D'AUTOMNE

The 1910 Salon d'Automne was also extremely important to the development of the coming Modernist style in France. It was at this exhibition that an invitation was extended by the exhibition's jury to the Munich Deutscher Werkbund in the hope that German participation would shake French designers and manufacturers out of the lethargy apparent in their recent work. The Munich exhibit – represented by the work of Thedor Veil, Adalbert Niemeyer, Paul Wenz, Richard Riemerschmid, Otto Baur, Karl Bertsch and Richard Berndl, among others – was intended to inspire the Germans' French counterparts to develop a new and distinctive national style.

Although French cabinetmakers and designers had by 1910 rejected the organic protrusions on Art Nouveau furniture in

*Left: Rose Adler designed this table of ebony, sharkskin, metal and enamel for couturier Jacques Doucet in 1926.*

*Left: a five-piece giltwood and Beauvais tapestry drawing-room suite by French designer Maurice Dufrêne.*

*Below: a massive, pallissander-veneered bar inlaid with mother of pearl and various stained woods. It is attributed to Jules Leleu, who favoured such floral designs.*

favour of a more restrained and functional style, they were not prepared to forego the Belle Epoque's preoccupation with lavish materials. Exotic woods, such as Macassar ebony, rosewood and amboyna, became fashionable, often veneered in patterns that accentuated their contrasting textures. Distinctive grains, such as those found in burl maple and calamander, added to the aura of opulence sought.

## FURNITURE EMBELLISHMENT

For large surface areas, designers embellished and sometimes even entirely covered furniture with such exotic materials as mother of pearl, sharkskin (known as shagreen and *galuchat*), parchment, snakeskin, gold and silver leaf, crushed-eggshell lacquer and ivory. These might form a pattern – usually stylised flowers or a geometric motif – or they might take advantage of the nature of the substance itself, perhaps using the imbrication pattern of the shark's skin decoratively. The shapes of furniture ranged from overtly traditional – eighteenth-century *bureau plats*, petite ladies' desks, *gondole* or *bergère* chairs – to more strikingly *moderne*, severely rectilinear with not a curve in sight.

*Right: Emile-Jacques Ruhlmann created this girl's room, which was included in Jean Badovici's* Intérieurs Français *in 1925.*

Other readily identifiable Modernist images, such as the sunburst, zigzag and chevron, likewise made their entry into the new grammar of decorative ornament before and during World War I in the work of André Mare and Louis Süe, two Parisian interior designers who formed a partnership in 1919. The period was characterised by experimentation, as artists and furniture designers searched for a means to distance themselves from the *fin de siècle* and to create a bona-fide twentieth-century style. In this, neo-classicism became a unifying force.

### DEVELOPING TRENDS

Indeed, when viewed retrospectively, there were two distinct trends within Art Deco furniture design. On the one hand, there were the early experiments in what we have now come to recognise as modern furniture, using metals and plastics in forms which could lead to eventual mass production, and on the other the high-quality craftsmanship of which Emile-Jacques Ruhlmann was the greatest exponent. An almost limitless number of French designers applied themselves to the Modernist style. For simplification, the furniture designers of the period can be grouped loosely into three broad categories: traditionalists, Modernists and individualists.

### THE TRADITIONALISTS

The traditionalists took France's eighteenth- and early-nineteenth-century cabinet-making heritage as their point of departure . This unimpeachable legacy provided the inspiration for a host of 1920s' designers, most importantly:

Emile-Jacques Ruhlmann, Paul Follot, André Groult, Jules Leleu, Louis Süe and André Mare, Armand-Albert Rateau, Jean-Michel Frank, Henri Rapin, Maurice Dufrène, Léon and Maurice Jallot, Eric Bagge, Georges de Bardyère, Gabriel Englinger, Fernand Nathan, Jean Pascaud, René Gabriel, Marcel Guillemard, Suzanne Guiguichon, Blanch-J Klotz, Lucie Renaudot, Charlotte Chaucet-Guilleré, Georges Renouvin, Pierre Lahalle and Georges Levard, Auguste-Victor Fabre, Pierre-Paul Montagnac, Alfred Porteneuve and the ageing 1900 *maître*, Louis Majorelle. In addition, most of the cabinet-makers in Paris's furniture-making quarter, the Faubourg Saint-Antoine, generated a range of proven, rather traditional, models. Mercier Frères and Saddier et fils produced some good-quality furniture

*Left: a chiffonier created in around 1926 by Emile-Jacques Ruhlmann. Veneered in amboyna, the inlaid pattern is of ivory.*

*Below: a decorated* cabinet bombe *in the* Japoniste *style by Clément Mère, a partner in the Süe and Mare collaboration.*

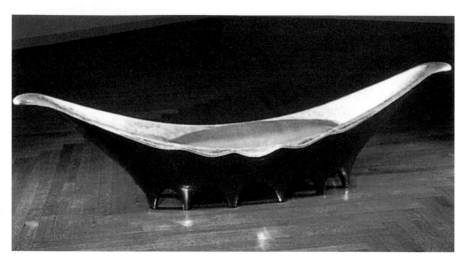

*Above: this lacquered and silver-leafed* pirogue *(canoe) sofa was made in around 1919–20 by designer Eileen Gray.*

*Right: a bench created by Eileen Gray from in around 1923. The model was made in various woods.*

in the modern idiom, as did André Frechet at the Ecole Boulle.

The achievement of the traditionalists was to re-evaluate the traditional furniture styles, take the best and subtly alter and revamp them. Many of the people responsible for furniture design were not themselves great craftsmen, but they were capable of running large workshops and using the talents of their own and other studios' craftsmen to best effect. They were virtuoso performers and they showed off their abilities to the utmost.

## EMILE-JACQUES RUHLMANN

Emile-Jacques Ruhlmann (1879-1933) was without peer as a cabinet-maker. A strict traditionalist, his forms were elegant, refined and – above all – simple and sleekly modern in their decoration and detail. His cabinets, desks, tables and chairs were veneered in costly, warm woods, such as amaranth, amboyna, ebony and violet wood, and embellished with silk tassels and subtle touches of ivory in dentate, dotted or diamond patterns. The long, slender legs – sometimes torpedo shaped with cut facets – were often capped with metal *sabots*, or shoes, a concept that was both decorative and practical.

The 1925 Exposition catapulted Ruhlmann to the front of the modern French decorative-arts movement. Until then, he had been known only to an exclusive and wealthy clientele. His pavilion at the Exposition, L'Hôtel du Collectionneur, would change that, however. Hundreds of thousands of visitors flocked through its monumental doors to gaze in awe at the majestic interior. Ruhlmann reacted with remarkable equanimity to the post-1925 advent of metal into furniture design, in view of the fact that much of his great reputation rested on the use of sumptuous veneers. He adjusted bravely to metal's advances, incorporating chrome and silvered metal into his designs, when many of his furniture forms became quite rectilinear; at the same time, his ivory dots and silk fringes gave way to chrome fittings, leather cushions and swivel bases.

Many of Ruhlmann's contemporaries generated superior furniture. Among the finest were Süe et Mare, whom Jean Badovici described as 'an admirable association of two dissimilar minds which combined the best of their qualities to put them at the service of Beauty. One provides a sure and precise knowledge and a rigorous sense of geometry; the other a refined and delicate sensibility'. The result was a highly distinctive and lavish range of furnishings inspired by the Louis XIV, Louis XV, *Restauration* and Louis-Philippe periods.

## THE MODERNISTS

The Modernists rebelled against the tightness of the neo-classical harness, bringing their own blend of individualism – defiant or understated – to the projects at hand. For these, metal was *de rigueur.* The most notable modernists were Jacques Adnet, Edouard-Joseph Djo-Bourgeois, André-Leon Arbus, Robert Block, Pierre Petit, René Prou, Louis Sognot, Charlotte Alix, Michel Dufet, Maurice Barret, Léon Bouchet, Georges Champion, Renée Kinsbourg, Maurice Matet and Paul Dupré-Lafon. These were joined towards 1930 by architects, who moved increasingly into the field of furniture design. René Herbst, Robert Mallet-Stevens, Jean Burkhalter, Pierre Chareau, André Luráat, Le Corbusier, Charlotte Perriand and Jean-Charles Moreux – to name only the most prominent – extended their architectural designs to the building's interior space and furnishings, giving prestige and authority to the Modernist philosophy. Le Corbusier's best-known furniture pieces, for

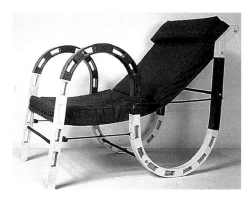

*Above: this wood and canvas armchair dates from around 1938 and was designed by the versatile Eileen Gray.*

*Left: Pierre Legrain and Jean Dunand collaborated on this red-lacquered cabinet commissioned by Jacques Doucet.*

*Right: a jungle confrontation is depicted on a lacquer and ivory screen by Jean Dunand from a design by Paul Jouave.*

*Below: a table by Jean Dunand. Red lacquer squares embellish the table; note the mass of* coquille d'oeuf *on the top.*

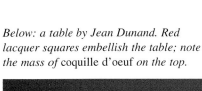

example, are his chaise-longues and chairs, often fashioned of tubular-steel frames and with simple but comfortable leather seats, designed in collaboration with his cousin Pierre Jeanneret and Charlotte Perriand.

The third group of furniture designers, that of the individualist, relates to those individuals whose brilliance and range of influences defy ready categorisation. Only four qualify: Pierre Legrain, with his bizarre blend of tribal African and Modernist influences; Irish-born Eileen Gray, with her lacquered Orientalism, whimsy, theatricality and Modernism; Eugène Printz, whose distinctly personal and kinetic designs were constructed in the traditional manner; and Marcel Coard, whose innovative spirit was allowed only an infrequent escape from the bulk of his more traditional and constrained decorating commissions.

## EILEEN GRAY

Eileen Gray (1879-1933) started out fashioning exquisite handmade objects, such as screens, tables and chairs. These were often embellished with Japanese lacquer, whose technique she studied with the master, Sougawara. Eventually she moved on to more rectilinear and strongly functional furniture, as well as to architecture. For *modiste* Suzanne Talbot she designed a Paris apartment between 1919 and 1920 which included a canoe-shaped chaise-longue in patinated bronze lacquer with subtle scalloped edges and a base comprising 12 rounded arches. By 1927, however, her chair designs were radically different and distinctly *moderne*. A padded-leather-seat *Transat* armchair, set on a rigid lacquer frame with chromed-steel connecting elements, was more akin to Le Corbusier than to Ruhlmann *et al.* Her case pieces, with built-in cupboards that feature swivelling drawers and doors set on tracks, and tables that moved easily on wheels, were considerably more practical.

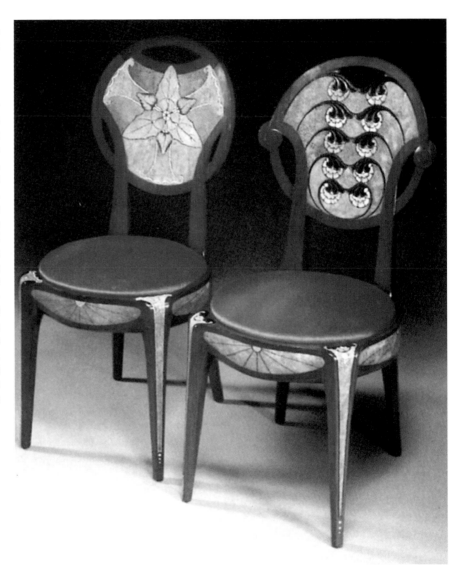

*Left: an occasional table by Clément Rousseau in exotic woods, shagreen, ivory and mother of pearl, c.1921.*

*Above: a pair of chairs by Clément Rousseau. Their frames are rosewood, their predominant material sharkskin.*

*Right: The elegant surface of this table by Pierre Chareau dating from around 1928 comprises palissander-wood veneer and an etched-glass top. Note the horizontal and vertical directions of the veneer.*

Pierre Legrain (1887-1929) initially made his mark as a designer of book covers for his wealthy patron Jacques Doucet. One of his most famous pieces of furniture was the *Zebra* chair, or chaise-longue. His clear affinity with all things African could hardly have been made more explicit than in this piece made in 1925. Compared to such representations of the opposite extreme of Art Deco as Eileen Gray's experiments in metals, Legrain's is nothing short of bizarre. The zebra skin is imitated in velvet, the armrest is decorated on the reverse with abstract patterns expensively executed in mother of pearl. The arm rest is left open from the front in order to house a small shelf whose purpose could be nothing more than aesthetic. The overall design is almost crude, appearing both clumsy and uncomfortable, but exudes a sensuous feeling of gratuitous luxury and decadence.

Among other important furniture designers in Paris was Jean Dunand (1877-1942), who mixed traditional lacquerwork with modern, angular forms. He was known for his *dinanderie* (the art of chasing and hammering metal) and for his lacquerwork, and also designed and decorated elaborate furniture, including cabinets, panels and screens. Indeed, lacquer exponents tended to concentrate their production on screens and *panneaux décoratifs*; for example, Gaston Suisse, Gaston Priou and Katsu Hamanaka. Dunand's pieces were often covered with figural or animal designs, either by Dunand himself or after a noted artist.

Dunand's pieces themselves may have been designed by an *ébéniste* such as Ruhlmann. His huge screens, often made of silver, gold and black lacquer, displayed huge geometric motifs, exotic Oriental or African maidens, lush landscapes or elaborate mythological scenes. His most famous piece was a bed made in 1930 for Mme Bertholet, in lacquer and mother of pearl.

### ROUSSEAU AND CHANAUX

Two artisans emerged as masters of Modernist materials. The first was Clément Rousseau, who designed and executed finely detailed furniture and precious objects in rare woods, toiled and stained leather, carved ivory and enamel. The other was Adolphe Chanaux, a virtuoso craftsman who executed furniture designs for André Groult, Emile-Jacques Ruhlmann and Jean-Michel Frank, as well as for his own creations. Chanaux's importance lay in his mastery of all of the period's most exotic and fashionable furniture materials – sharkskin, parchment, vellum, ivory, straw marquetry and hand-sewn leather – to which he applied his talents with equal facility.

In summary, no unified furniture aesthetic had emerged at the 1925 Paris Exposition. Rather, there was an uneasy coexistence of contradictory images and styles. Varnished rosewood appeared alongside tubular nickelled or chrome steel; the Cubist rose competed with Constructionist geometry; and the brilliant colours derived from the Ballets Russes and the Fauves clashed with the subdued tints used by Modernists who preferred achromatism.

Just as there had been a transitional period between the Art Nouveau and Art Deco periods, so there was a gradual progression from high-style Art Deco to Modernism during the late 1920s.

### THE UNION DES ARTISTES MODERNES

In 1930, a new organisation was formed to give identity to the group of designers who took Modernism as their doctrine: the Union des Artistes Modernes (UAM). Members included René Herbst, Francis Jourdain, Hélène Henri, Robert Mallet-Stevens, Pierre Chareau, Raymond Templier, Edouard-Joseph Djo-Bourgeois, Eileen Gray, Le Corbusier and Charlotte Perriand. These Modernist architects

and designers rejected the ornamentation characteristic of the early 1920s, giving priority to function over form. They designed furniture in materials such as steel, chrome and painted-metal tubes, in which individual elements were designed for mass production.

### INDUSTRIAL MATERIALS

As simplicity became increasingly fashionable, furniture designers working in the high Art Deco style had to combine their traditional forms with industrial methods and materials. In glass, René Lalique extended the traditional uses of the medium in his designs for a series of tables and consoles. Wrought iron was another material used in furniture manufacture

*Left: the dining table and chairs are of glass and chromed metal. The table features inlaid panels by René Lalique.*

*Right: this elegant
and luxurious
bathroom was
designed by
Armand-Albert
Rateau for Jeanne
Lanvin between
1920 and 1922.*

during the 1920s by such leading proponents as Edgar Brandt, Raymond Subes, Michel and Jules Nics, Paul Kiss, Adelbert Szabo and Richard Desvallières. By the end of the decade, wood had practically disappeared from the furniture shown at the annual salons. The glorious age of France's *ébénistes* had passed.

## JACQUES DOUCET'S PATRONAGE

The first patron of the new Modernist style was the couturier Jacques Doucet, who in 1912 commissioned Paul Iribe to design and furnish his new apartment on the Avenue du Bois, Paris. Doucet sold his collection of eighteenth-century furniture and *objets d'art* at auction, replacing it with contemporary paintings and

furnishings. In the same year, Paul Poiret, also well known as a fashion designer, established his Atelier Martine. In 1924, Doucet again sought Modernist designers to decorate the studio which he had commissioned the architect Paul Ruau to design for him in Neuilly to house his collection of Oceanic and African art. Pierre Legrain, who had worked for Paul Iribe during Doucet's earlier commission, was joined in Neuilly by a cross-section of Paris' most avant-garde artist-designers: Eileen Gray, Marcel Coard, André Groult, Rose Adler, Constantin Brancusi, Paul Mergier and also Louis Marcoussis.

Another celebrated couturière and art patron, Jeanne Lanvin, retained Armand-Albert

Rateau to decorate her house and boutique, and Madeleine Vionnet commissioned Jean Dunand similarly to furnish her house with his lacquered furniture. His patinated-bronze, wood and marble furnishings were rife with elaborate floral and animal motifs – birds supporting a bronze coffee table; deer amid foliage on a bathroom bas-relief; marguerites entwining a dressing table. While Rateau's furniture and overall vision are among the most figurative and truly sculptural of the period, the heavily veneered, embellished and/or lacquered pieces of many of the others are much more handsome and restrained, often deriving from classical shapes. Classical scrolls, or *volutes*, were used to decorate furniture, as well as stylised wings, animals, birds and human figures.

### THE PARISIAN DEPARTMENT STORES

Expensive and élitist as the luxury trade undoubtedly was, its resurgence depended on other factors. Apart from a few specialist shops, the outlet for contemporary furniture was limited. When the new department stores realised that design could be of great use to them, the situation altered.

During the inter-war years, Paris home-owners could select their furniture from four major department stores – Au Printemps, Le Louvre, Au Bon Marché and Les Galeries Lafayette. A fifth, Trois Quartiers, was established in 1929. The function of these stores was that of arbiter of taste, especially in the promotion of modern household commodities. To serve their clients better, the stores established their own art studios in which to design and manufacture what they believed the customers wanted, rather than what they had previously been forced to accept through lack of choice. The studio for Au Printemps was Primavera; that of Le Louvre, Studium Louvre; that of Au Bon Marché, Pomone; and that of Les Galeries Lafayette, La Maîtrise. The cream of France's young designers – Louis Sognot, René Prou, Robert Block and Etienne Kohlmann – were brought in to direct these studios and modern furniture production. The public was easily persuaded that it was, at long last, getting what it wanted: modern furniture at a reasonable price.

Competition between the department stores spread to smaller firms, such as René Joubert and Philippe Petit's Décoration Intérieure

*Below: a bizarre bronze and marble table by Armand-Albert Rateau, with four stylised birds used as supports.*

*Right: a design for a young man's bedroom by M Guillemard, furnished by Primavera.*

*Below: a DIM jewellery cabinet decorated with Chinese red lacquer and* coquille d'oeuf, *1926.*

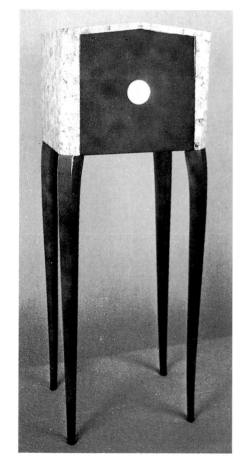

Moderne (DIM); André Domin and Marcel Genevrière's Dominique; Michel Dufet's Meubles Artistiques Modernes (MAM); and Louis Süe and André Mare's La Compagnie des Arts Français. Furniture benefited from the competition, as designs and materials were modernised. At the 1925 Exposition, both the stores and firms were well placed to present a wide range of ultra-modern household goods to the public.

### ART DECO FURNITURE REASSESSED
Art Deco furniture is certainly one of the most interesting and inspired applications of the style. The high prices it commands nowadays

are certainly due to its rarity, but they also reflect another factor: that of the value of quality craftsmanship. Even when Ruhlmann sold his furniture during the 1920s, such pieces were only affordable by the wealthiest of wealthy clients. If his work commanded high prices, it was not because of commercial greed but because of the months of skilled labour and the use of the most expensive materials as expressions of his genius. If such a piece of furniture were to be copied today, it would be next to impossible to find a cabinet-maker who would be capable of producing it. The 1920s and 1930s witnessed, among so many things, the dying of the old crafts.

# NON-GALLIC
# ART DECO
# FURNITURE

By the end of the 1920s, much tubular-steel furniture was being created both by architects and furniture designers. The public was asked to reconsider the aesthetic merits of utilitarian, even humble materials, such as steel and metal alloys, for furniture production. Metal entered the home through the kitchen door – in the traditional manufacture of metal household utensils – after which it gradually worked its way into the other rooms of the house. Final and complete acceptance came in the selection of metal rather than wood for salon and dining-room furniture. In between the elegantly carved and veneered confections of high-style Art Deco and the near-antithetical, ultra-*moderne* tubular-steel and leather creations of Le Corbusier and others were myriad pieces of furniture designed by Europeans that reflected either – at times even both – of the Art Deco design schools, with the occasional unique and completely innovative design making its own waves.

*Preceding page: De Stijl designer Gerrit Rietveld's* Red and Blue Chair *of 1918 has become an icon of modern design.*

*Above: A living-room suite designed by Félix Del Marle in 1926 for 'Madame B'.*

The infiltration of Modernist furniture into the home and office was not just restricted to France. It had, in fact, developed more quickly in more progressive countries. Germany is often considered the pioneering nation in the development of the modern movement. The Belgian designer Henry van der Velde founded the Weimar School of Applied Arts in 1906, which was absorbed in 1919 by Walter Gropius who, in turn, founded the Bauhaus. This was an attempt to unify all the myriad of disciplines within the decorative arts under the general direction of architecture.

### THE BAUHAUS
The Bauhaus instructors and their students advocated rational and functional design, and an increased dependence on the machine for mass-production. One of the most important Bauhaus furniture designers was Marcel Breuer who, with Mart Stam and Ludwig Mies van der Rohe, was the first developer of the

cantilevered tubular-metal chair. Later, in England, Breuer explored further the use of industrial materials in his design for a laminated plywood lounge chair, manufactured by the Isokon Furniture Company in London.

### THE PRAZSKE UMELECKE DILNY
New developments in Eastern Europe reflected a similar adherence to the new Modernist philosophy. In Prague, the Prazske Umelecke Dilny (Prague Art Shop) had been founded in 1912. Leaders of this school included Pavel Janak, Josef Chocol, Vlatislav Hofman and Josef Gocar, who designed furniture inspired by the Cubism of Braque and Picasso, and some of whom believed that only a designer's artistic concepts were important, and that technical and functional aspects of design were secondary. The outbreak of World War I put an end to the endeavour.

Although most critics view German design of the 1920s in the context of the Modernism

*Above: the Finnish architect and designer Alvar Aalto created this bent, laminated wood chair and blocky sideboard.*

*Right: the Russian-born architect/designer Serge Chermayeff designed this walnut- and coromandel-veneered sideboard while working for the British furniture-makers Waring & Gillow.*

*Below: a British coffee table, c.1930, veneered with peach-coloured mirror glass.*

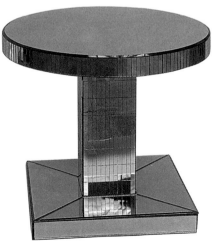

embodied by the Bauhaus, many German designers now considered Modernists actually created furniture in the contemporary French style. Bruno Paul, of the Munich Vereinigte Werkstätten and director of the Berlin Kunstgewerbeschule, for example, invariably incorporated an element of richness into his furniture designs. He tried to update German Baroque traditions, and while his veneered pieces were often embellished with ivory knobs and finials like Ruhlmann's, his forms were more awkward and less sleek, the legs more serpentine than gently tapering. Well into the 1920s, he continued to design pieces in luxurious materials and with thick, glossy veneers for the Deutscher Werkbund, a group known

for its emphasis on the union of artists and industry. The furniture designed by Paul for the 1927 Cologne Exhibition was more in keeping with the Modernist high style in Paris than the machine ethics of the Bauhaus.

## VENEERING AND FINISHING

German designers like Bruno Paul thus made expensive, custom-made furniture in limited quantities. According to one contemporary commentator, 'Special attention is paid here to the wood used and to the finish. The simpler and more severe the piece the more attention is paid to the materials. Especially handsome inlaid pieces are preferred because it is possible by clever assembling of veneers to achieve beautiful patterns'. That observation drew an obvious comparison with the well-crafted and sumptuous cabinetry of France's foremost designers, such as Ruhlmann and Leleu, who also catered to an elite clientele.

## DE STIJL

In The Netherlands, the de Stijl group was formed in 1917. Theo van Doesburg, Gerrit Rietveld and Félix Del Marle designed furniture intended to fill the Utopian interior spaces conceived by the leaders of the movement, Piet Mondrian and van Doesburg. Their furniture was angular and skeletal, of simple construction, employing planar, wooden boards painted either black or in the primary colours favoured by de Stijl artists. Architect-

designer Gerrit Rietveld created his famous *Rood Blauwe Stoel* (*Red and Blue Chair*) in 1918. Just as the de Stijl movement's painters combined simple geometric shapes, primary colours and horizontal and vertical lines in their canvases, so this classic chair combined these same primary ingredients in a three-dimensional manner; the final result may have been uncomfortable, but it has none the less become an icon of modern design.

## SCANDINAVIAN FURNITURE

French-inspired furniture was also produced in Scandinavia, and by the late 1920s the functionalism championed by the Bauhaus had begun to assert itself. This influence was felt the most strongly in Sweden, which was more

*Above: an elegant chaise-longue designed by Betty Joel, a proponent of functional and easy-to-care-for furniture.*

*Left: Sir Edward Maufe designed this desk for the 1925 Paris Exhibition. It is made of champhor, mahogany and gilded ebony.*

receptive to avant-garde German ideology than its neighbours. Erik Gunnar Asplund was perhaps the premier Scandinavian designer to work in the Modernist style. He designed an armchair made of mahogany, leather and ivory in around 1925, produced by David Blomberg of Stockholm, in a style which evoked the Paris fashion. The chair was part of a suite of furniture favourably reviewed by the critics at the 1925 Exposition.

Some of the Bauhaus' most fruitful and artistic ideas were evident in furniture shown at the landmark 1930 Stockholm Exhibition held at the Nordiska Kompaniet (NK) department store. The exhibition revealed a revolutionary attitude to domestic design, with special emphasis on residential architecture and furnishings. In keeping with modern concerns for practicality, flexibility and hygiene, dwellings at the exhibition had large windows, light walls and a minimum of furnishings. The furniture was geometrical in shape and extremely light, with restrained decoration.

### BRUNO MATHSSON

The new furniture forms developed by the Bauhaus architects had a profound impact on international design by the 1930s. Noteworthy were Breuer's bent tubular-steel models, which were imitated, albeit with modifications, throughout Europe. In Scandinavia, however, designers preferred to incorporate Breuer's functionalism with traditional materials, such as wood, in serial production. Bruno Mathsson is probably the best-known Swedish designer of the period. One of his notable furniture

*Right: this lavish table and chairs were created by Joseph Urban in around 1921.*

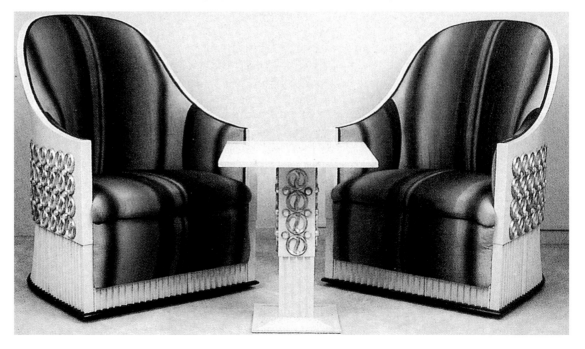

designs was the *Eva* chair of 1934, produced by the Firma Karl Mathsson in Varnamo. Made of bent beech upholstered in woven fabric, the model was sculpturally moulded to fit the human body. Mathsson's experiments in bent and laminated wood, also combined with his studies of function and maximum comfort, generated many popular designs which have remained in continuous production since their conception several decades ago.

### DANISH DESIGNERS

At the same time, designers in Denmark moved into new areas of experimentation. Kaare Klint made furniture which combined practicality with economy. His first independent commission was to design exhibition cases and seats for the Thorwaldsen Museum of Decorative Arts in Copenhagen. His *Red Chair*, designed in 1927 for the museum, was widely acclaimed.

Alvar Aalto began to design modern furniture during the 1920s. His *Scroll* or *Paimio* armchair of around 1929 has become a classic of modern Finnish design. The frame and seat are made of laminated and painted bentwood. The model captures the qualities of functionalism and lightness sought in tubular-metal furniture, adding a pleasing note of grace in its use of natural wood and sinuous curves. Aalto's bent- and laminated-wood stacking stools of 1930-33, produced by Korhonen in Turku, were also very successful commercially due to their formal simplicity and inexpensiveness. The stools have remained entirely practical and adaptable to multiple requirements in the variants produced later.

### DESIGNERS IN STEEL

Other Scandinavian designers also experimented with tubular steel. In 1929, Herman

*Left: Paul T Frankl's* Skyscraper *bookcase/cabinet, made from birch and lacquer in about 1928. Frankl was the first US designer to embrace the skyscraper as a decorative motif.*

*Above: two 'skyscraper' chests of drawers made of ebony-trimmed walnut designed by Paul T Frankl, c.1928.*

Munthe-Kaas of Norway designed an armchair produced by the Christiania Jernsengfabrikk of Oslo. Although its form is based on Breuer's tubular-steel prototype, the model differs in its incorporation of an unusual metal-strap back and a series of simple string hooks that support the upholstered seat.

### BRITISH FURNITURE

In Britain, which had a strong native tradition of solid Arts and Crafts-style furniture, craftsmen such as Edward Barnsley designed rectilinear, sturdy pieces that bore no similarity whatsoever to *moderne* continental designs. Others, however, such as Betty Joel, Ambrose Heal, the Russian-born Serge Ivan Chermayeff, Gordon Russell and the design firm PEL (Practical Equipment Limited) produced functionalist furniture with distinctly modern lines and – especially in the case of Chermayeff – occasional stylised-floral pieces. Chermayeff, who trained initially as an artist in Paris, has been credited with the introduction of the modern movement into Britain. His chromium-plated metal tubular furniture and unit storage systems represented a dramatic departure from the sterile, tradition-bound models of his adopted country.

### THE INFLUENCE OF JOHN ROGERS

Along with Chermayeff, the designer John C Rogers was instrumental in bringing the modern style to England. In an article in the *DIA Journal*, Rogers had begun as early as 1914 to instil a new spirit of design into British industry. He pleaded for a national conversion to Modernism and for a final rejection of the Arts and Crafts philosophy. In 1931, he visited the Bauhaus in Dessau with Jack Pritchard and Wells Coates, a trip which inspired the furniture he exhibited at Dorland

Hall, London, two years later. In 1932, in collaboration with Raymond McGrath and Coates, Rogers redesigned the interior of the BBC; he later emigrated to the United States. Coates also designed modern furniture during the 1930s for PEL, including notably an ebonised-wood and chromium-plated metal desk inspired by an earlier Breuer model.

### THE INFILTRATION OF THE AVANT-GARDE

The general absence of furniture in England in the Modernist style was thus punctuated by a handful of spirited avant-garde models. Sir Edward Maufe, an architect known principally for Guildford Cathedral, designed a range of furniture that appears to have been inspired by Paris. A typical example is provided by a desk manufactured by W Rowcliffe in around 1924, exhibited at the 1925 Exposition. Made of mahogany, camphor and ebony gessoed and gilded with white gold, the desk had all the sumptuousness and ostentation characteristic of prominent French models.

Russell designed a boot cupboard in 1925 in Honduras mahogany in a style very similar to French models introduced a few years earlier. And in 1929 Heal produced a desk and chair in weathered oak on which the perpendicular detailing again betrayed the influence of contemporary continental models.

### BETTY JOEL

At the end of World War I Betty Joel and her husband established their decorating firm in South Hayling, with a showroom in Sloane Street in London. Early designs revealed the fact that she was self-taught. By the end of

*Right: Paul T Frankl's man's cabinet and mirror, c.1938. Silver- and gold-plated metal half moons enhance the doors.*

the 1920s, however, she had developed a distinctive furniture style in which curved contours (described by her as silhouettes of the female form) predominated. Superfluous mouldings and projections were eliminated; ornamentation was achieved through a range of luxurious, contrasting veneers.

Joel's firm won many commissions to decorate libraries, boardrooms, shops and hotels, and many of her designs were popularised by English manufacturers of modestly priced furnishings. She retired in 1937 and is primarily remembered today for an inexpensive line of furniture aimed at the working woman.

**THE UNITED STATES**
Although Paris was across the Atlantic, it was

*Below: a red-lacquered 'puzzle' desk, embellished with silver, by Paul T Frankl.*

not too far for its influence to be felt in the United States. American designers were well aware of the prevailing Modernist style in Paris through periodicals of the day, and through a succession of exhibitions that travelled across the country during the second half of the 1920s. A loan exhibition of items from the 1925 Exposition opened at the Museum of Fine Arts, Boston, in January 1926, from where it proceeded to the Metropolitan Museum of Art, New York, and six other American cities.

### THE FRENCH INFLUENCE

Correspondingly, attempts were occasionally made to introduce a flamboyant European style of furniture, some noteworthy. The Company of Mastercraftsmen in New York, for example, produced shameless copies of contemporary French models, replete with marquetry panels and ivory trim. Joseph Urban, an Austrian architect better known as a designer of stage and cinema sets, likewise designed somewhat theatrical furniture, such as a table and armchair, made around 1920, both of classical proportions and adorned with mother-of-pearl inlays, manufactured by the Mallin Furniture Factory.

### AMERICAN MODERNISM

In general, however, the high Parisian style of the 1925 Exposition was rejected by the public, which viewed it as a Gallic eccentricity too exuberant for traditional local tastes. And, when Modernism established itself in America during the late 1920s, it was the strain of northern European machine-made, mass-produced metal furniture which found acceptance.

Paul Frankl, whose 1930 cry 'Ornament = crime' was taken up by a good many *moderne* American designers, is known primarily for his skyscraper furniture, inspired by the

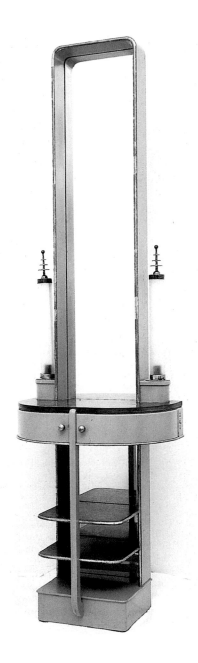

*Left: a side table designed by Kem Weber for the Bissingers. The piece is made of burl walnut, glass, silvered and painted wood, chromium-plated metal, maple and cedar.*

*Above: an armchair in Macassar ebony by Kem Weber, probably designed for the Kaufmann department store, c.1928.*

recesses on the tall buildings which soared above his New York gallery. He also created a man's cabinet and series of 'puzzle' desks that incorporated materials and finishes found on contemporary French models: red and black lacquer, gold- and silver-plated metal, and gold and silver leaf.

### SKYSCRAPER STYLE

The German national Karl Emanuel (Kem) Weber and J B Peters, two Los Angeles designers, also adapted the skyscraper style to their tall pieces, and Chicagoan Abel Faidy produced a leather settee with a whimsical design derived from architecture for a private penthouse apartment which could easily have been custom-built for Radio City or the Chrysler Building, or else some equally contemporary complex. Weber was trapped in California at the outbreak of World War I.

Refused permission to return to his homeland, he finally settled in Los Angeles, where he joined the design studio at Barker Bros as a draughtsman. In 1927 he opened his own design studio in Hollywood, listing himself as an industrial designer. Not only was Weber virtually the only decorative-arts designer to embrace the Modernist creed on the West Coast, but his style was highly distinctive. For the John W Bissinger residence in San Francisco Weber created a striking suite of green-painted bedroom furniture enhanced with Hollywood-type decorative metal accents.

### FRANK LLOYD WRIGHT

The metal and wood furniture of Frank Lloyd Wright was not as severe as that of the Bauhaus school. For instance, his renowned 1936-39 desk and chair, called *Cherokee Red* and designed for the S C Johnson & Son building in Racine,

*Right:* Cherokee Red *desk and chair, 1936-39, by Frank Lloyd Wright for S C Johnson & Son.*

Wisconsin, have their steel frames enamelled in a warm, russet-brown tone which complements the American walnut of the chair arms and desk top, as well as the chair's brown-toned upholstery. The two pieces are an essay on the circle, oval and line – and are undoubtedly far more inviting to an office worker than, for example, the shiny chrome-and-black leather pieces of Breuer *et al*.

### AN AMERICAN MIXTURE

Eliel Saarinen, Eugene Schoen, Wolfgang Hoffmann (the son of the Viennese Josef Hoffmann, and an American emigrant), Gilbert Rohde and Joseph Urban were among the many designers who applied their talents to creating furniture for the American market. On the whole, their pieces were sturdy, mass-produced and distinctly Modernist, some echoing French, German and Viennese design, others uniquely American in their form, colour and materials. Aluminium, chromium and other metal furniture was in the ascendancy, but the wooden pieces continued to thrive, with veneers of native woods such as holly, birch, burr maple and walnut handsomely covering large surface areas.

### ELIEL SAARINEN

One of the finest Modernist furniture designers in the United States was Eliel Saarinen, a native of Finland. For his own house at Michigan's Cranbrook Academy, Saarinen designed a dining-room ensemble which drew on the principles of French Modernist design. The chairs have classically fluted backs emphasised by the contrasting colours of the pale fir veneer and the intersecting black-painted vertical stripes. The accompanying table is inlaid with an elegant geometrical pattern which recalls the restrained parquetry designs

*Left: an oak side chair (c.1916-22) designed by Frank Lloyd Wright for the Imperial Hotel in Tokyo.*

*Right: a vintage photograph of the 'Great Workroom' of the S C Johnson Building in Racine designed by Frank Lloyd Wright. Note the smart desk and chair sets.*

introduced by Dominique and DIM in Paris some years earlier.

Eugene Schoen, a native of New York, also created furniture in a restrained Modernist style. After visiting the 1925 Exposition, he established his own interior-decorating firm in Manhattan. Some of his more notable models, manufactured by Schmied, Hungate & Kotzian, betrayed a strong French influence in such details as their Directoire-style sabre legs and fluted backs.

### MASS-PRODUCTION

Many designers in the United States created Modernist wood furniture, much of it manufactured in the industry's principal centre, Grand Rapids, Michigan, by firms such as Berkey & Gay, the Johnson-Handley-Johnson Company and the Imperial Furniture Company.

Included were Herman Rosse, Ilonka Karasz, Jules Bouy, Herbert Lippmann, Ely Jacques Kahn, Robert Locher, Winold Reiss and Norman Bel Geddes. Furniture manufacturers like the Herman Miller Furniture Co in Zeeland, Michigan, the Troy Sunshade Co in Troy, Ohio, and the Ypsilanti Reed Furniture Co, in Ionia, Michigan, retained designers such as these to provide them with models for their lines of mass-produced furniture.

### DONALD DESKEY

In metal furniture, Donald Deskey emerged as the country's premier designer, combining the luxury of French Modernism with the technology of the Bauhaus. Perhaps one of the finest examples of his work was his dining table for the Abby Rockefeller Milton apartment, between 1933 and 1934. Although the piece included a Macassar-ebony top, it was the inclusion of new materials – polished chrome and glass, and the siting of a bulb beneath the top to provide dramatic lighting effects – that drew the critics' praise.

For his interiors for the Radio City music hall in 1932, Deskey set convention aside in a display of ostentation intended to buoy the Depression-wracked nation seeking refuge in films and live entertainment. The private apartment above the music hall which Deskey designed for its impresario, Roxy Rothafel, was even more lavish.

Several other designers in the United States created excellent metal furniture during the late 1920s and 1930s, in particular Gilbert

*Below: an executive suite consisting of a desk, chair and lamps designed for S L Rothafel by Donald Deskey.*

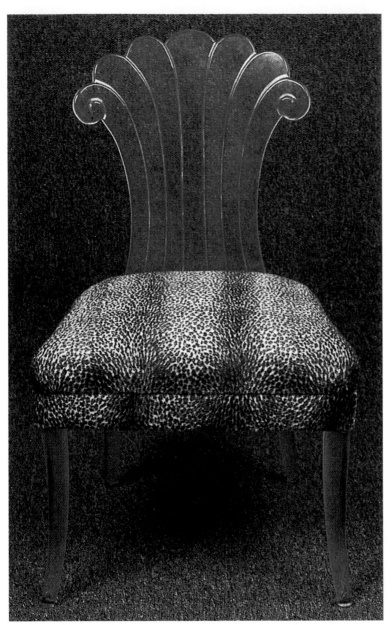

Rohde, Wolfgang and Pola Hoffmann, Warren McArthur, Walter Dorwin Teague, and the lighting specialist Walter von Nessen. Walter Kantack, a New York metalware manufacturer, also produced inspired metal pieces of furniture, as did the architect William Lescaze, of Howe and Lescaze.

## A GLITZY STYLE

At the far end of the spectrum was T H Robsjohn-Gibbings of California, who worked in a luxurious and fiercely anachronistic neo-classical style which greatly appealed to his wealthy clients in the showbusiness community. Classical motifs such as scrolls, palmettes, lyres, rams ' heads and hoofed feet adorned his tables, mirrors and chairs, pieces which were mostly made of parcel-gilt carved wood and gilt-bronze.

## THE ADVENT OF NEW MATERIALS

By the mid-1930s, it was evident that metal had won the battle with wood for the domestic American furniture market. Whereas wood was still preferred in some sectors of the household market, metal increasingly began to win adherents. By then, such synthetic materials as Formica and Lucite were already being used in furniture design, with an armchair by Elsie de Wolfe, in a traditional, scrolled-back design of moulded Lucite, demonstrating a strange but witty meeting of the old and the new.

*Left: a side chair created for Hope Hampton by Elsie de Wolfe, c.1939. What makes the chair astonishing is the use of Lucite for the 'traditional' back and legs.*

# ART DECO
# METALWORK

*Above: a pair of doors covered in monel metal adorn the lobby of New York's First National City Trust Co.*

*Right: a slender copper vase created by Jean Dunand, c.1920-25. It has been gilded and patinated.*

*Preceding page: this bronze grille in the style of Brandt is from the Circle Tower Building, Indianapolis, completed in 1938.*

The history of Art Deco metalwork is also that of changing materials. The 1920s was the period of wrought iron, bronze and copper. By the early 1930s, these had not been completely replaced, but designers favoured the more modern aluminium, steel and chrome. Adaptability and inventiveness flourished in Art Deco metalwork. Metal was often used on its own for gates and doors, but it could also be employed in conjunction with almost any of the other favoured materials. The 1930s were remarkable, not only for any single colour preference, but for the lack of any colour at all. Glass and shiny metals complemented each other; both were reflecting and anonymous, sparkling and transparent. The typical 1930s' room had mirrored walls, with discreet metal borders, repeated in the bent-metal furniture. There were no distractions, except for their own reflections. Such stark ideas were a long way from those involved in the initial resurgence of metalwork.

Art Deco metalwork pieces ranged from the intimacy of a commemorative medallion or a small mantelpiece clock to the huge entrance gates for the 1925 Exposition. As wrought iron has few limitations beyond that of the craftsman's skill, it broke through the confines of use in one specific area. New developments in technology made wrought iron indispensable where any type of scientific innovation introduced into the home or building required decorative camouflage. Radiators cried out to be covered, and wrought iron was ideal for this purpose because it neither obstructed the flow of heated air, nor was it adversely affected by it. Lift cages became decorative focuses in building lobbies, co-ordinated in design with railings and entrance doors to create an overall unity that was modern, practical and stunning in its impact. The combination of wrought iron

with other metals, such as copper, silver, bronze, steel and aluminium expanded the opportunities for memorable, dramatic and unusual decorative effects.

### SUBJECT MATTER IN METALWORK

In general, the Art Deco movement was broadly defined by two predominant styles. The first and most strongly 'traditional' made use of stylisations of nature: of birds, flowers and animals; natural phenomena such as clouds, waterfalls and sunbursts were also subject to varying degrees of geometrification. An almost Mannerist elongation of proportions and an exaggeration of round volumes were also much in evidence, and there was a predilection for choosing those animals and plants as subjects that naturally exhibited some of these qualities. Greyhounds, gazelles, pigeons and ripe fruit were among the motifs that came to be associated with Art Deco style. After 1925, wrought iron also began to reflect in its images the more simplified geometric lines of the 'rationalists', as well as the sleek lines of machinery, aeroplanes and steamships. The beauty of the straight line had thus become the new aesthetic.

## THE DOMINANCE OF PARIS

Art Deco metalwork was dominated by Parisian designers, notably Edgar Brandt, Jean Dunand and Jean Puiforcat. They worked in three entirely different manners, however, each producing a distinctive metalwork style which inspired designers in France, the rest of Europe and the United States.

## JEAN DUNAND AND JEAN PUIFORCAT

Jean Dunand (1877-1942) was a designer *extraordinaire* who trained first as a sculptor. He directed his talents to various mediums, but finally made his name in lacquerwork, applying the coloured resin to wood and metal surfaces and creating jewellery, bookbindings, vases, tables, panels, screens and mantelpieces of the utmost beauty. Jean Puiforcat (1897-1945) also worked in metal, and his stunning creations in silver and silver-gilt, often with semi-precious stone and glass embellishments, occupy a unique place in Art Deco design.

## THE FRENCH STYLE

Other French metalworkers included Raymond Subes, Paul Kiss, Armand-Albert Rateau, Louis Sognot and Nics Frères. Their console tables, lighting fixtures, grilles, doors and screens were beautifully executed and featured various motifs from the Art Deco repertory. Pierre-Paul Montagnac and Gaston-Etienne le Bourgeois, a painter and sculptor respectively, successfully allied modernity and tradition in wrought-iron design. But in the end it was Brandt's *oeuvre* that set the standard, not only

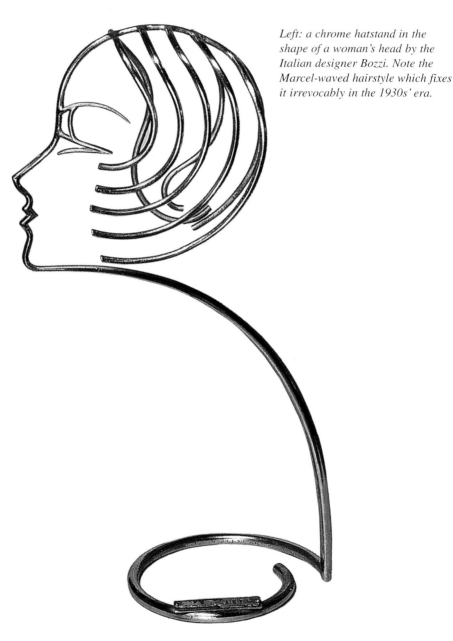

*Left: a chrome hatstand in the shape of a woman's head by the Italian designer Bozzi. Note the Marcel-waved hairstyle which fixes it irrevocably in the 1930s' era.*

*Right: a pair of andirons crafted in wrought iron by Edgar Brandt during the early 1920s, when the serpent was a popular decorative motif.*

*Below: this lift door, 1927-28, once adorned Selfridge's store in London. Edgar Brandt designed the wrought-iron and bronze panel.*

for French, but also for other European and American ironwork as well.

### EDGAR BRANDT

Brandt (1880-1960) was an ironworker of immense talent and breadth who created jewellery, vases, lamps and firedogs, as well as grilles, doors, panels and screens. He often collaborated with architects and glassmakers, as at the 1925 Paris Exposition, where his several successful exhibits gained him worldwide recognition. His designs – executed in copper, bronze, gold and silver – often combined animal and human forms with floral and/or geometric patterns. Many of his surfaces were hammered in a decorative manner, as that of a lovely bronze platter which featured seaweed and other marine motifs. Brandt's most popular designs by far featured attractive human and animal forms, usually in openwork floral or foliated surrounds. He also made small andirons in the shape of cobras and jardinières with cobra handles. (The snake, taken from Egyptian art, was a popular Art Deco subject, also used by Jean Dunand, René Lalique, François-Emile Décorchement and others.)

### BRANDT'S COLLABORATIONS

Through his father's involvement in an engineering firm, Brandt had early on developed an interest in working with metal. Most of his early work came from direct commissions by architects who needed metal fixtures for private houses and hotels. Brandt never lost his willingness to work with others, and, indeed, his best work was almost always the result of direct collaboration.

Many of his commissions demanded a highly developed sense of detail and the ability to work to a very strict set of limitations. At the same time as he was creating pairs of

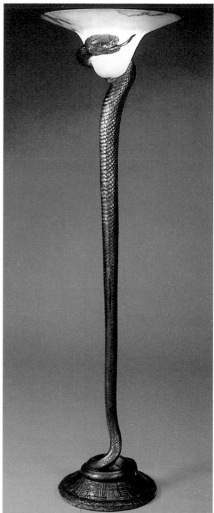

*Left: a detail from Edgar Brandt's* L'Oasis *five-panel screen.*

*Below: the* La Tentation *floor lamp, designed by Brandt and Daum frères.*

*Right: Classical* volutes *figure on this hammered wrought-iron urn by Edgar Brandt.*

monumental doors, or wrought-iron staircases for the liners *Paris, Ile de France* and *Normandie*, Brandt would be designing more mundane pieces: grilles for indoor heating, radiator covers and other everyday objects. Some of his finest work was with the glass expert Antoine Daum. His cobra standard lamp, the coiling serpent acting as a foot, stem and holder for its Daum glass shade, is among one of his most striking creations.

Brandt had a deep respect for the aesthetic and moral heritage of French art, and saw it as his duty to keep France in the forefront of contemporary decorative design. He felt that industrial processes could be well used to serve this end, and sought constantly to ally art with industry. Many artists feared that the intro-duction of industrial techniques would lead

to mass-production which, they felt, would debase their art, but Brandt found this fear groundless. It was his conviction that artists could only benefit from an understanding of the mysteries and difficulties of production and also of the techniques of the machines.

## THE 1925 EXPOSITION

He had himself served a long apprenticeship, not only in wrought-iron working, but also in silversmithing and jewellery-making, for which he had won prizes at the salons of the Société des Artistes Français. A man of phe-nomenal drive and energy, he executed both his own designs and those of others.

Although already well known before 1925, it was Brandt's varied and extensive work shown at the 1925 Exhibition that catapulted

him to the forefront of his field. He was com-missioned, with Ventre and Favier, to design the Porte d'Honneur (the gate of honour) for the Exposition, which they designed in col-laboration with René Lalique and Henri Navarre. The Porte d'Honneur was made of a 'staff', an inexpensive alloy, for the cost of iron in a project of this size and imperma-nence was prohibitive. Part of the challenge was to make the 'staff' look as fine as the ma-terial which it imitated. It was a great success, as were the other commissions that he carried out for the Exhibition. In particular, he was responsible for the acclaimed metal furniture and furnishings for the Ruhlmann pavilion. Another vital exhibit was his own pavilion, for which he designed an *ensemble* that included the spectacular and monumental five-panel screen *L'Oasis*, a highly refined fantasy of stylised flowers, foliage and fountains executed in brass and iron.

## FERROBRANDT INC

The Brandt *ensemble* led to his first major commission in the United States, for what is known as either the Madison-Belmont or the Cheney Building, on the corner of Madison Avenue and 34th Street in Manhattan, where the exterior metalwork is still *in situ*. Cheney Brothers, a fabric house that occupied several floors in the building, also invited him to design their showrooms. This gave him the impetus to open Ferrobrandt Inc in New York. He expanded his operations in Paris at the same time, taking full advantage of all the publicity that evolved from his work at the Exposition.

## BRANDT'S TECHNIQUE

His work was successful because Brandt understood the delicate balance between the monumental and the decorative. His extraordinary talent for balancing these two elements added great style to modern decoration. He was sometimes criticised for his use of industrial techniques, but his work was always redeemed by the beauty of the material, his meticulous attention to detail, and especially by the fine finished appearance of his pieces. This finish was achieved by an industrial technique that he perfected – oxyacetylene welding, which is all but invisible. In joining decorative elements, Brandt used hidden screws and bolts so that the eye was never distracted by details of construction.

Brandt exploited the tensile strengths of the material he used when designing furniture. Console tables, instead of standing solidly on four squat legs, could be treated more as open sculptures. Legs would be opened out with delicate filigree mouldings of fans and thistles filling the gaps, yet would still have enough strength to support the heavy weight of a thick slab of marble. Fire screens and doors could be reinterpreted to look almost like drawings suspended in air. Curling lines and leaves in door fronts seemed exquisitely delicate but had a strength and solidity fit for their purpose. Brandt also collaborated with Henri Favier on a series of decorative screens for which he provided the framework.

## A COHESIVE STYLE

Another reason for the great success of Brandt's

*Above: a wrought-iron table with a massive top of grey granite that is attributed to Raymond Subes.*

*Left: Raymond Subes designed this suite in bronze, wrought iron, marble and corduroy.*

*Above: an elaborately decorated hall stand, pedestal and wall sconces crafted in wrought iron by the naturalised French designer Paul Kiss in around 1925.*

designs was his understanding of the relationship of each individual piece, such as a grille, staircase or chandelier, within an *ensemble* to the whole. Further objects designed by Brandt – including trays, paperknives, pendants, brooches, as well as other small items of jewellery – are testimony to the same inventiveness and sureness of hand that characterise his more monumental works.

### RAYMOND SUBES

Raymond Subes was second only to Brandt in the scope and quality of his work. In 1919, at a relatively young age, he was appointed successor to Emile Robert as the director of the firm of Borderel et Robert.

Subes endeavoured to create an impression of richness and elegance in his work, but with great simplicity of technique. This aim was completely in accord with the economic and social conditions of the time, for the public demanded the maximum effect for the lowest price. Subes' solution was similar to that arrived at by Brandt: the marriage of artistic design to industrial technique. He found through his research that industrial processes could be used with very satisfactory results both in furniture and in more massive architectural works. This philosophy journeyed a long way from that of his mentor, Emile Robert, who had stubbornly scorned the use of anything but hand-held tools.

Subes devoted a great deal of time to the technical problems of his trade: how to produce the finest work, restrict costs as far as possible, and yet maintain artistic integrity. He aimed much of his research particularly at the uses of sheet metal, which could be formed by machine into any desired shape. Subes was also ingenious at using flat iron pieces to create works in series. Using

*Left: an exotic bronze chair concocted by Armand-Albert Rateau. Apart from its cushion, it is awash with marine motifs.*

*Below: a silvered-bronze medallion made by Foucault and applied to an amboyna-wood veneered cabinet by Ruhlmann.*

*Above: the door of the Gulf Building in Houston is influenced by Edgar Brandt.*

machines, Subes was able to produce pieces as cheaply as by casting. At the same time he understood that unique pieces must still be produced by hand, and he himself often took up the hammer to create powerful bas-reliefs for a door. A new type of metalwork had been born which allowed for production in series, and also made possible works too monumental to be executed at the forge.

## PAUL KISS

Paul Kiss was born in Romania, but after studying in Paris became a naturalised Frenchman. His work explored the lyrical and expressive qualities that he saw in wrought iron, but was quite different in character to that of Brandt, with whom he collaborated early in his career. He exhibited a comprehensive range of wrought-iron furniture and lighting at the salons of the Société des Artistes Décorateurs and the Société des Artistes Français.

## NICS FRÈRES

Jules and Michel Nics were Hungarian-born brothers who worked in Paris under the name of Nics Frères, producing a complete range of decorative ironwork, from furniture to architectural decoration. Their work was characterised by a highly conspicuous *martelé* (hand-hammered) decorative finish and a rather excessive use of natural forms, even after these had gone out of fashion. They rejected as heresy die-stamping and file work, and affirmed themselves as masters of the hammer, proud of their ability to make any piece by hand in a technique comparable to that of the finest artisans of the past.

Although Brandt was clearly the leader of the more traditional metalworkers, men like Subes, Adnet, Kiss, Rateau and Szabo produced work of great beauty. The most eccentric of this group by far was Armand-Albert Rateau. He constructed a bronze chaise-longue for Jeanne Lanvin's boudoir that rested, almost comically, on the backs of four deer. A washstand and mirror piece was modelled from two peacocks standing back to back, their two heads holding the mirror.

With metal, anything was possible, but the bizarre examples of Rateau were way out of keeping with the clean and practical furniture of Le Corbusier or Eileen Gray. Elegance was not just the domain of the intricate foliage of a Brandt screen, a Kiss cabinet or a Subes mantelpiece clock: it could be seen to even greater effect in an oak table top supported by just two sheets of bent metal by Louis Sognot. It was minimal, reduced to the contrast between the two materials used: the shiny, cold metal and the rich patina and grain of the wood.

There were also various Art Deco medallists working in silver, bronze and other materials, not only in France but also in Britain, Germany and the United States. The Hungarian-born Tony Szirmai, who was based in Paris, specialised in commemorative pieces;

Pierre Turin produced silver, copper and bronzed-metal plaques, often octagonal, which featured stylised figures and flowers; while André Lavrillier created a handsome medal depicting Leda and the swan.

### BAUHAUS METALWORKERS
At the Bauhaus, Wilhelm Wagenfeld, an architect and industrial designer, was especially associated with the metal workshop from 1922 to about 1931, when he left to work with glass and ceramics. He fashioned a hammered-copper coffee machine in 1923 which is so futuristic in appearance that it could be a prototype for an astronaut's helmet.

Marianne Brandt of the Bauhaus is, however, perhaps the best-known German metalworker. Surprisingly, she turned her supreme design skills to rather mundane objects, such as ashtrays, shaving mirrors and cooking utensils. The most famous is her *Kandem* bedside lamp, which, with its push-button switch and adjustable reflector/shade, is the forerunner of so many similar lamps today.

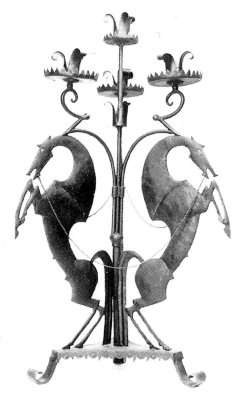

*Above: a wrought-iron candelabrum made by William Hunt Diederich during the 1920s. His work was characterised by its sharp, silhouetted imagery.*

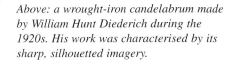

*Left: a Zephyr digital clock designed by Kem Weber for Lawson, Time, Inc, c.1933.*

*Above: Monel metal sheathes a lift interior at Unilever House, London. The panels on the right depict modern transportation.*

*Right: a four-tubed bud vase, which was mass-produced in various metals by Chase Brass & Copper Co of Connecticut.*

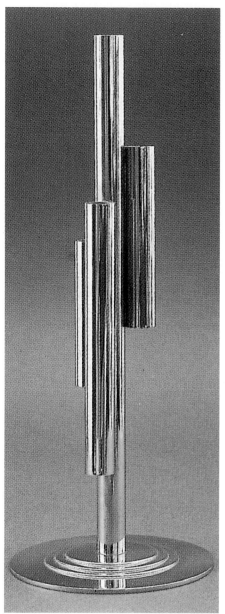

## AMERICAN METALWORK

Although the United States lagged behind France in its adoption of metalwork for interiors, the influence of the 1925 Paris Exposition and the opening of Edgar Brandt's New York office stimulated a taste for this highly versatile area of the decorative arts. By the late 1920s, it had become immensely popular, and there were a number of American designers and craftsmen who were producing a great variety of both interior and exterior ironwork.

Large-scale metalwork in America – gates, architectural elements and such – were much influenced by the Parisian designs of Brandt, Subes and other *ferronniers*. Their impact can be clearly discerned on the designers at the Rose Iron Works in Cleveland, Ohio, whose screens and tables are blatant imitations of Brandt's works.

## OSCAR BACH

Oscar Bach was perhaps the only craftsman in this field who could match the technical mastery of the great French ironworkers. Born in Germany, he enjoyed a successful career there before coming to the United States in 1914. He opened a studio in New York, where he was soon flooded with private and commercial commissions. Proficient in many metals and styles of metalwork, he used copper, aluminium, bronze, chrome and nickel silver to provide colour and textural contrast in the decorative elements he designed. His contribution to many of New York's most outstanding buildings is immeasurable.

Other noted American metalworkers included William Hunt Diederich and Kem Weber. William Hunt Diederich emigrated to the United States from Hungary when he was 15 and took up residence in Boston with his grandfather, William Morris Hunt, who was an artist. Diederich was a successful designer in many areas, but was particularly attracted to metalwork. His simple, two-dimensional figures and animals seem snipped out of iron. With their sharp, jagged edges and minimal surface decoration they have a lively vitality that reflects their creator's personality and love of animal subjects.

In contrast, Weber's designs for clocks (including digital ones in the 1930s), lamps, tea and coffee sets, as well as furniture. were sleekly functional. Even the smallest of items, such as a stepped clock case of brass and chromed metal, was impeccably designed and undeniably 'machine age'.

## COMMERCIAL METALWORK

Further Modernist influences can be seen in the designs of the Chase Brass & Copper Company in Waterbury, Connecticut, which employed famous as well as obscure designers. It produced a wide range of useful wares known for their 'beautility' – cigarette boxes, ashtrays, cocktail shakers, wine coolers, kitchen utensils, candlesticks and vases. Its designs were wonderfully *moderne*, architectonic, Cubist and crisp. A bud vase of 1936, for example, consists of four chrome pipes that are attached to each other at uneven angles and rest on a circular base.

Many American metalworkers were engaged in gigantic architectural projects for which they often turned to materials other than the traditional iron, bronze, brass and copper. Aluminium, chromium, cadmium and 'monel' metal (a nickel-copper alloy), among others,

*Right: a radiator grille designed by Jacques Delamarre for New York's Chanin Building, 1929, that reproduces in brass the exterior of the building.*

*Àbove: a tiled executive bathroom in the Chanin Building in New York. Its decoration was supervised by Jacques Delamarre and the geometric motifs that adorn it echo the details of the building's metalwork features (see page 61).*

all came into play, sometimes used as thin sheetings (or plates) over another metal. Numerous components of New York skyscrapers – elevators, mail boxes, doors and so on – were made of these new metals, used either on their own or in combination with other materials. Some of these (often anonymous) creations, with their geometric, floral and figural grillework, have come to be considered among the most outstanding examples of Art Deco in the United States, and can be seen in New York's Chanin and Daily News buildings, as well as in countless other structures throughout the country.

### DINANDERIE

Yet it was not only new, non-precious metals with which designers worked – a number of whom were proficient in *dinanderie* (named after the Flemish town of Dinant). Many of the techniques of metal encrustation were of ancient origin, and by returning to old traditions and reinterpreting them differently, twentieth-century artists were able to produce works of a singular vitality.

The interest in Japanese art that began during the late nineteenth century had much to do with the resurgence of interest in *dinanderie*, as well as in lacquer. Jean Dunand, who was to become the most important artist to work in both these techniques, was introduced to the medium by the Japanese lacquerer Sougawara. He quickly mastered the technique of lacquering and his fascination with this and *dinanderie* produced some of the most extraordinary objects of his, or any other, time. Obviously the lacquer had to be applied to a surface, and Dunand began with vases, all made by hand in the *dinanderie* technique. His earliest vases derived their shape from gourds and other vegetal forms, and he often worked the surfaces with repoussé, chiselling, patinas of browns and greens and inlays of other metals either to highlight the naturalistic form or to produce such organically inspired motifs as scales and peacock feathers. His forms gradually became simpler and his designs more geometric, relying on surface ornamentation and applied metal for effect.

### GOULDEN, FAURÉ AND LINOSSIER

Jean Goulden created clocks, lamps, boxes and other *objets* in metal, often embellished with coloured enamelling, a process he learned from Dunand, with whom he sometimes collaborated. His avant-garde, highly angular works often resembled Cubist and Constructivist sculpture. Camille Fauré also worked with enamel on metal, but, unlike Goulden's pieces, his vessels were dominated by the coloured enamel.

Claudius Linossier was a master of the art of *dinanderie*, who had been an apprentice metalworker in his native Lyons when only 13 years old, and had mastered embossing, engraving, enamelling, metal encrustation, repoussé and all the other metalwork techniques. The most outstanding element of his work is his use of metal encrustation. He loved the subtle play of one tone against another, and as silver and copper provided only a limited palette, he began to develop his own alloys, using ingots he cast himself, and fashioning thin plaquettes that he graded by tone.

### SERRIÈRE AND MERGIER

Another silversmith who occasionally worked in base metals, often with silver inlays, was Jean Serrière. His objects, mainly trays and bowls, are massive in feeling and of extremely simple design, enlivened by traces of the hand work that formed them. Paul-Louis Mergier,

*Above: A lampshade with a beaten-metal* dinanderie *base made by the versatile designer Jean Dunand.*

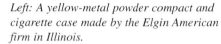

*Left: A yellow-metal powder compact and cigarette case made by the Elgin American firm in Illinois.*

an aeronautical engineer who painted, designed and made furniture, also found time for *dinanderie* work. His vases are simple in form, and his preferred subjects were stylised figures and animals defined by various patinas, inlaid silver and lacquer, often executed by the well-known Japanese artist Hamanaka.

### DAURAT'S PEWTER

Maurice Daurat was an artist who chose to work in pewter. Pewter is a soft metal, ductile and extremely supple, and Daurat exploited its almost flesh-like surface and its potential for sombre shadows and irregular reflections of light from hammer marks, finding that these imparted a warmth more appealing than the cold gleam of silver. His designs became increasingly refined until they were almost a series of exercises in form and simplicity. His minimal concessions to ornament were a ring of beads at the base, or an interestingly designed handle. He intended his pieces to be admired rather than used, and in his hand pewter indeed achieved the status of a new-found material and could stand next to the finest silver without shame.

*Above: A jewel-like, enamel-on-copper vase by Camille Fauré.*

*Right: A silver and jade soup tureen created by Jean Puiforcat.*

# ART DECO
# FASHION AND
# JEWELLERY

# A
# FASHIONABLE
# STYLE

Art Deco survives today as the last truly sumptuous style, an extremely fertile chapter in the history of the applied arts. Art Deco is essentially a style used for the applied arts, though most of its sources are in the fine arts, architecture, as well as sculpture and painting. It was the first truly twentieth-century style which was international. Arriving when it did, it was a style that could be adapted to every man-made object. It also arrived at a time when new forms of communication would ensure its rapid spread. Finally, and most importantly, it was the last total style.

The term 'Art Deco', which derives from the Exposition des Arts Décoratifs et Industriels, held in Paris in 1925, is used to describe, in somewhat simplified terms, the many diverse developments that took place in the world of design between the two wars. It is, however, an apt title for the artistic style that followed on immediately from Art Nouveau at the end of the nineteenth century. The latter had relied on floral motifs to pattern and ornament its artefacts, whereas Art Deco was thoroughly modern in turning away from the winding, sinuous qualities of Art Nouveau, looking instead to those of abstract design and colour

*Above: a hand-tinted postcard advertising the 1925 Exposition Internationale des Arts Décoratifs et Industriels in Paris.*

*Opposite: an American powder compact decorated with a handsome geometric motif dating from the late 1930s.*

MINISTÈRE DU COMMERCE ET DE L'INDUSTRIE

# PARIS · 1925

EXPOSITION
INTERNATIONALE
DES ARTS DÉCORATIFS
ET INDUSTRIELS
MODERNES
AVRIL - OCTOBRE

IMPRIMERIE DE VAUGIRARD-PARIS

for colour's sake; and, when turning to nature for inspiration, it preferred to portray animals, or the beauties of the female form. Where Art Nouveau had been heavy, complex and crowded, Art Deco was clean and pure. The lines in Art Deco did not swirl around like the centre of a whirlpool; if they curved, they were gradual and sweeping, following a fine arc; if they were straight, they were straight as a ruler. Art Deco could be light-hearted on one level and deadly serious and practical on another. As the style in a time of unprecedented change, it was fluid enough to reflect that change.

## CHANGES IN FASHION

The style which later became known as Art Deco traces its origins to the period before World War I. In the first decade of the twentieth century, many factors caused an abrupt change in fashion. The couturier Paul Poiret, for example, revolutionised dress design, freeing the female form from constricting layers of clothing. Serge Diaghilev's performances of the Ballets Russes in Paris in 1909 and in the United States in 1916 provided another influence, both through their introduction of bright colours into the drab world of fashion, and their emphasis on the Orient. New art movements, such as Cubism, Futurism and neo-plasticism, helped further to create a new vernacular for art, which in turn initiated new concepts in jewellery design that were taken up with renewed interest after World War I.

## THE STYLE OF THE NEW

The spirit of Art Deco was the spirit of the modern. Even though it adapted older styles for its own use, it was still the style of the

*Left: A French poster designed for the 1925 Paris Exposition by Robert Bonfils.*

new. It was the style of the age that wouldn't stay still and looked to that age for its content, its meaning and often its subject matter. Art Deco may have been the modern style, but it emerged from as many different directions as it had applications. Art Deco was given its greatest cohesion in the Exposition of 1925, in a city that was also the Paris of Pablo Picasso, Georges Braque, Fernand Léger ad Robert and Sonia Delauney. Such Art Deco pieces as a decorated cigarette lighter by Gérard Sandoz could not have come from any time earlier than 1910.

### THE PARISIAN INFLUENCE

Paris was the stage on which almost all the battles of modern art were fought. The rapidity with which style has since followed on style has made it almost impossible to discern any lasting direction today. From Impressionism through post-Impressionism, Symbolism, Cubism, Futurism, Orphism, Constructivism, Purism, Surrealism, Vorticism, one 'ism' has replaced the next with disarming regularity.

### THE TREND TOWARDS ABSTRACTION

What many of these 'isms' had in common, which would be of great importance to Art Deco, was that they shared a tendency towards abstraction, moving away from more obvious subject matter towards a concern for the basic elements of picture-making or sculpting, so that form, colour, line and volume became important in themselves. The artist's feelings and sensibility could be read, it was hoped, through the manipulation of those infinitely flexible variables. As for the decorative arts

*Right: The fantastically popular Josephine Baker adopts one of the exaggerated poses that were popular with Art Deco sculptors.*

129

*Far right: an ivory and bronze bust by an anonymous sculptor. The subject wears an elaborately decorated cloche hat.*

*Right: this enamelled metal powder compact is a souvenir of the Empire State Building and dates from the 1930s.*

in the Art Deco style, they ranged from the purely functional, through simple and clear decoration, to pure ornament. That is why it is impossible to talk of one Art Deco style: there were as many directions, hybrids and strains as there were practitioners. The easiest way to understand and unravel the puzzle is to see where Art Deco came from and what sources it may have used.

### THE EMERGENCE OF THE AVANT-GARDE
When Picasso and Braque set off together in 1907 on the journey through their radical discoveries that would lead to Cubism, they turned art, as it had then been understood, on its head. The shock waves pulsed across Europe into

Russia, and across to North America in less than five years. Out of Picasso, abstraction had been born. The process of art had become a search, an experiment. Modernism came into being, and the avant-garde was invented. It had become viable, and ultimately necessary, to test out all the infinite options, to play intellectual games, and to extend and expand the boundaries of art. To be ahead of one's time, or at least up there with it, pushing forward, was to be a modernist. Like-minded designers could apply these principles to the decorative arts and arrive at something wholly novel. In a lesser way, they could apply the colour schemes of a Mondrian painting, a Goncharova, El Lissitzky, a Wyndham Lewis, or simpler

still, a Malevich, and arrive at simplicity itself. In the transition from fine art to applied art, the most simple motif had passed from being shocking, avant-garde and bewildering, to being accepted and merely decorative.

### ART NOUVEAU AND PRIMITIVE ART
Art Nouveau was of central importance to the rise of Art Deco, if only as a style to react against. Equally, Hoffman, Olbrich, Peche and Moser, who founded the Wiener Werkstätte at the beginning of the century, were early practitioners of a style which, when refined, looked like very early Art Deco. Another influence, which probably became the most important of all, was a response to primitive art. What

had happened throughout the late nineteenth century was a reappraisal of primitive art. Anything that was not European was recognised as having some artistic worth. Indeed, Europe looked away from the products of a diseased society that had chosen to massacre its youth across the battlefields of the Somme, to an art that was primitive, untouched and natural. This was particularly relevant to Art Deco, because by the time the style began to develop, a tendency towards the primitive was not just an option, it was obligatory.

### THE BALLETS RUSSES

Nobody looking back at Paris in the first quarter of this century could ignore the impact of the Ballets Russes on the arts. Driven by its passionate Svengali and impresario, Serge Diaghilev, its stage designs and costumes mixed the Oriental with the Westernized, the avant-garde with the primitive. Léon Bakst, its most famous designer, produced costumes whose lavishness and exotic Orientalism came as a complete shock to the Parisian public. Diaghilev's production of *Scheherezade* was a riot of deep, rich colour, which would inspire the heavier, decorative side of Art Deco and interior design.

### ERTÉ'S SET DESIGNS

Even more ambitious in the Art Deco style were the thousands of gouache drawings for set designs of Erté. The sinuous, sweeping curves of dresses and curtains fell across a rigidly simple, but still evocative, backdrop. Elegantly arched windows looked in on novel interiors bedecked with leopard-skin rugs and abstract, rectilinear furniture, enlivened by

*Left: Poster advertising the Grand Bal de Nuit, designed by Natalia Gontcharova.*

*Right:* Powder compacts, both bejewelled and non-precious, were produced in vast quantities during the 1920s and 1930s.

*Below:* Pearls, and Things and Palm Beach, a watercolour by Emil J Bisttram.

dancers in Oriental costume. That was part of Diaghilev's legacy to Art Deco. If that was not enough, he also incorporated the latest in contemporary dance, design and music.

If Oriental art had been made fashionable by the Ballets Russes, Mexican, Egyptian, North American Indian and South American art was of equal importance. What Art Deco learned, and then taught the public, was bold design. If colours were to be bright, they should knock you over; if lines were to be clear, they should be as stark and severe as the steps up a temple. The obvious could be chic. Indeed, if any one trend could be said to characterise the 1920s and 1930s it must be the way in which innovation was constantly and rapidly transmuted into chic. The radical tendencies and advances in art, architecture and design were fast subsumed into the broad arena of public consumption, into such disparate and far-flung areas as transportation, politics and mass communication.

## THE AFTERMATH OF WORLD WAR I

Prior to these two decades, the West had been effectively destroyed by World War I. But cataclysm became a catalyst for fundamental change: in the post-war world the desire for a fresh start, for a new epoch of progress and peace, became paramount. By the 1920s the world had changed politically. In Germany, the founding of the Weimar Republic in 1919 created a climate in which an institution such as the Bauhaus could operate. In Russia, the founding of the Union of Soviet Socialist Republics also had its repercussions on a worldwide scale. Later still, in Italy and Germany, the rise of

*Right: Limited edition lithograph and poster, designed by Jean Dupas in 1928.*

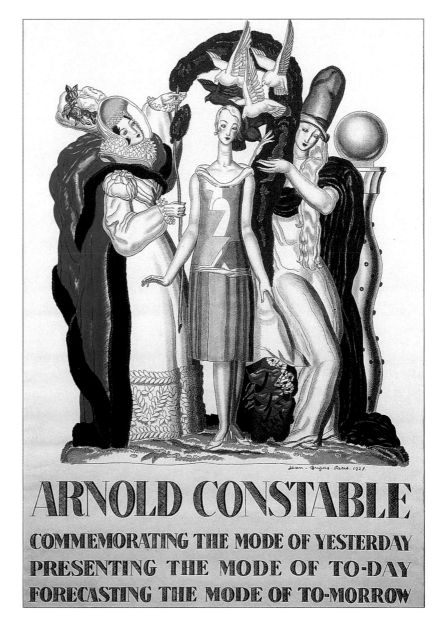

ARNOLD CONSTABLE

COMMEMORATING THE MODE OF YESTERDAY
PRESENTING THE MODE OF TO-DAY
FORECASTING THE MODE OF TO-MORROW

*Right: "Transatlantique" poster for*
Compagnie Générale Transatlantique, *1930s.*

fascism was set in opposition to communist ideas. The the world economic recession, the great slump and the Wall Street Crash contributed to the political and economic cocktail which helped to create the unique character of the Art Deco decades.

These were also truly international decades, for great international exhibitions (such as the 1925 Art Deco exhibition in Paris) at once aided the flow of ideas between continents, while paradoxically shoring up nationalist tendencies. Once every four years the Olympics performed the same functions, showing the world national displays and international co-operation.

World War I acted as a catalyst in other ways, too. The industrial world made advances far beyond those which would have been occasioned by five years of peace time. Aeronautics, medicine and industrial chemistry benefited from the effects of the 'war to end all wars'. Industry itself had found that it needed to develop extremely efficient mass-production techniques in order to cope with demand.

### MACHINE DESIGN

So the final, and one of the most obvious, influences on Art Deco was there to see at every street corner, in every house, factory and shop, on the sea, and also in the air. The twentieth century was the machine age. Art Deco was modern because it used aspects of machine design as inspiration: the wings of an aeroplane, the bow of a yacht, the porthole of the cabin window of the new ocean liners, the cogs and wheels of a sewing machine or a motorcar engine. It was even more modern because

*Right: An African couple drawn by George Barbier in 1920. The lush exoticism of Africa appealed to Art Deco designers, as did the delicate ornamentation of Asia.*

*Below: This detail of a Philadelphia diner illustrates how architects took the materials and forms of the industrial age and magnified them to architectural proportions.*

L'Afrique

NEW YORK DIRECT
O QUEBEC & MONTREAL

it accelerated the adoption of new materials such as plastic, Bakelite and chrome. And, while Art Deco upheld the importance of craftsmanship in the teeth of the new forms of mass production, it often benefited greatly from this development. Although Art Deco objects were originally made with expensive and rare materials, many ideas were copied and manufactured to provide cheaper alternatives for the less wealthy public.

**AN ALL-PERVASIVE STYLE**
Art Deco was therefore a style that spread through every aspect of daily life between the wars; every form of art and craft used the new sensibility, as is particularly reflected in the worlds of jewellery and fashion that are explored in this book.

*Above: two of Cunard's most famous liners, the* Queen Mary *and* Queen Elizabeth, *illustrated in Art Deco style in a poster dating from the 1950s.*

# ART DECO
# FASHION

The world of fashion, clothing and accessories is always quick to pick up on the latest changes in taste. The fashion that appeared during the 1920s and 1930s is well known to anyone who has ever looked at films of the period, and it is not difficult to build up an accurate, if superficial, overview of fashion during the 1920s and 1930s from the statuettes by Preiss, the photograph of Nancy Cunard in her African bangles, or photographs of Picasso, Jean Cocteau and others *flâneurs* and *poseurs*. Art Deco fashion has been repeated and diluted so many times since that it becomes difficult to place it historically, to see where it came from, or to notice how subtle modifications point to a dress being a 1960s' replica or the original.

*Right:* Match de Boxe (Boxing Match), *a fashion plate that appeared in the influential French fashion journal* Art, Goût, Beauté *in May 1923.*

*Preceding page: Portrait of Nancy Cunard by the society photographer Cecil Beaton.*

The reason for the rapid success of Art Deco was that it was essentially a fashionable style. All styles have their day, but in the twentieth century the fashion industry moved quicker in response to public taste than ever before. This has as much to do with built-in obsolescence as with a sense of style and finesse; both feed off each other. Tastes fluctuate quickly, so the industry has to come up with something new, as clients try to stay one step ahead of the rest of the pack. Then, as now, styles changed from season to season, with hemlines constantly fluctuating, waistlines appearing and disappearing, skirts growing slimmer or fuller. None the less, the great early Paris couturiers dramatically brought fashion to the fore, making it as influential as any other design medium, a circumstance that has remained constant in the six or seven decades since they first made their mark.

138

In itself, fashion may only be as important to people as the amount of care they take in clothing themselves. For the elegant Parisian or New Yorker of the 1920s and 1930s, fashion was a vital part of life. Fashion is always to do with snobbishness, and with Art Deco this was particularly important, since it was a total style. If your collector lived amongst Ruhlmann tables, Lalique sculptures, African chairs by Pierre Legrain, lights by Brandt and Daum, a coffee service by Sèvres or Clarice Cliff, place settings by Jean Puiforcat; if he or she lit your cigarette with a lighter designed

*Right: This cover for* La Sourire *was designed by the artist S. Zaliouk.*

*Below: A 1922 drawing from Art, Goût, Beauté of a model wearing a white crêpe cocktail dress by Worth.*

t - Beauté

*Right:* Kora, *a gilt- and gold-painted bronze and ivory figure of an exotic dancer by Demetre Chiparus.*

by Gérard Sandoz to the strains of Paul Robeson or a jazz number on the gramophone, then you could guarantee that the cut of the husband's suit, the length and sharpness of his lapels, the width of tie and the wife's dress by Schiaparelli would be precisely in keeping. If so much effort in intellect, taste and money had been expended on creating the home environment, then the only things that could travel out of the door (clothes and jewellery) had to be just as important; they had to complement the overall effect.

### THE STYLE OF THE AGE

There is a somewhat perverse rule in fashion that the poorer the economic climate for the majority of people, the more ostentatious the select, wealthy few become. The double standards of the 'Roaring Twenties', in the United States particularly, where Prohibition cast a depressing cloud of double-dealing, suspicion and crime, reflected itself in the androgynous short skirts, bob cuts and shapeless tops worn by the flappers. By the beginning of the 1930s, when the reality was far more depressing and the comforting stool of wealth had been kicked away from under the feet of the erstwhile bootleggers, the fashion became fuller, while the jewellery (even if it was paste) became even more startling.

Fashion played a very important role in Art Deco design, not only in terms of its direct influence on other mediums (the Ballets Russes costumes, for instance, made waves) but also because many of its leading lights, Paul Poiret, Jacques Doucet and Jeanne Lanvin among them, were extraordinary collectors and taste-makers who helped enormously to promote *Le Style 25*. In terms of design, the effect of fashion items on the other applications of Art Deco was fairly minimal; as a mirror to hold

Far left: Asian fashion as interpreted by George Barbier in an illustration dating from 1920.

Left: This Barbier stencil from La Gazette du Bon Ton shows a dancer in a low-waisted dress. The cap was a typical head-covering of the day.

up and see the speed of change reflected, however, fashion was unrivalled. Sometimes, of course, the converse was true. The statuettes and Chryselephantine figures of Otto Poerzl and Ferdinand Preiss were direct reflections of the opera and ballet costumes, as well as the ballroom clothes, of the period. They were knowing little nods; small, elegant gestures of recognition that the owner appreciated the essence of what it was to be fashionable.

## FASHION ILLUSTRATION

Fashion illustration was significant as well: for not only did the drawings of Paul Iribe, Georges Lepape, George Barbier and Erté help in themselves to spread the new couture, but furthermore, their styles and use of vivid colours had a strong influence on many other artists in France and across the world.

In Parisian fashion design, as in other mediums, the influence of the Ballets Russes was paramount. Serge Diaghilev's company had invaded the French capital in 1909, and its Oriental splendour – in costumes, scenery and dance itself – transformed the course of Gallic design. Almost immediately, Léon Bakst's exotic creations, his ornamental, brightly hued and sumptuous fabrics, began to be reflected in French couture. Colour, which had before been reduced to subdued shades in clothing, suddenly came alive with the Ballets Russes. Bakst's sets and costumes radiated with oranges, bright blues and greens, generating a sudden craze for anything Eastern.

At the same time the impact of Paul Poiret (1879–1944) was being felt as he brought this mania for the exotic into fashion, first by streamlining dresses and then by introducing the Empire waistline. Having started his career working for both Worth and Doucet, he had already begun to make his name by 1906, with his fluid dress designs distinguished by their smooth, corsetless line, which in effect liberated twentieth-century woman from the past. In 1908, Paul Iribe had produced a set of vividly coloured *pochoirs* (stencilled ink drawings) illustrating his new fashions, *Les Robes de Paul Poiret*. The bright colours and exotic, Oriental aspects of his fashions derived from his love of Indian and Persian art and his admiration for the Ballets Russes. His vivid creations, coupled with those of the Ballets Russes, heralded a new era, not only in design but in illustration as well. Preceding most

*Above: A Hindustan design by Paul Poiret from the* Gazette du Bon Ton, *1920.*

of Art Deco by at least a decade, they were very much in the forefront of the style.

## PAUL POIRET

Paul Poiret spread his influence and taste far wider than most of the other French fashion designers, for he was not only a dress designer. Indeed, he advanced the entire style with the workshop he founded in 1912, the Atelier Martine (named after his daughter), where he employed young working-class girls whose charming drawings and designs were the basis for rugs and carpets, upholstery and curtain fabrics, wallpapers, furniture, lamps, and even dolls, which he marketed through his Maison Martine. Whole interior-design schemes were the products of Poiret and his atelier, not only for his own residences but also for those of others. At the Exposition des Arts Décoratifs et Industriels Poiret exhibited his designs on decorated barges just under the Alexander III bridge. He was, above all, a patron of the arts and a man of true Art Deco taste, supporting young artists and also collecting their works, creating perfumes, publishing books, and holding fancy costume balls. When he needed an architect for his fashion house in Paris, he used the firm of Perret Frères. The entrance door to the premises was one of Edgar Brandt's masterpieces in metalwork. Poiret recognised the importance of creating a suitable environment in which to display his talents and impress his wealthy clientele.

## THE CHANGING ROLE OF WOMEN

World War I introduced women into the workforce, helping to liberate them further from constrictive clothing. For patriotic reasons, it became acceptable for women to undertake certain types of work previously barred to them. This change in the traditional role of women brought a sweeping transformation in what they wore. Furthermore, during World War I there was a need to conserve heavy fabrics for the troops, which hastened women's acceptance of a softer, slimmer silhouette. In 1917, Mrs Vernon Castle arrived in Paris and changed forever the concept of the ideal woman. Her slim, lithe figure glided across the dance floor, charming society with the latest ballroom dances and providing a preview of the energetic woman who appeared after the war to challenge the staidness of her predecessor's role in society. By the time the war ended in 1918, women had gained freedom in dress and were not about to give it up.

Poiret's slim, high-waisted dresses had been replaced in 1917 with a line of low-waisted models. Besides the straight, sleek, sometimes Empire-waisted dresses which liberated the Art Deco woman from painful corsets and bulky petticoats, she could be seen wearing exotic turbans, often bejewelled or plumed, small cloche hats and bandeaux perched above her eyebrows.

### THE NEW FASHIONS

By the end of World War I, hems were almost universally short (but still below the knee), and waists began to be dropped. Busts were de-emphasised, and backless dresses – declarations of freedom – abounded for evening. Colours were bright, often outrageously so, and patterns were bold, usually floral. Their hairstyles also reflected women's new, postwar independence, becoming short and cropped or 'bobbed'. Hemlines fluctuated for the first five years of the 1920s, from ankle to calf length. Then, in 1925, skirt hems shot up to just below the knee (the length associated with the 1920s today), and dropped back to mid-calf length in 1929. The silhouette of the body became long and flat and suppressed all curves. Both the neckline and the back of the dress fluctuated, the latter plunging to near-obscene depths. Making its appearance in the winter of 1923, the cloche hat (which became a symbol of the 1920s) completely covered the head from the eyebrows to the nape of the neck. Long hair, or hair pinned back in a bun, distorted the shape, however, which prompted women to cut their hair in the new, short styles. At the end of the decade, muffs were preferred over gloves to complement the now fashionable, fur-trimmed coats.

*Left:* Le Messager (The Messenger) *by Edouard Halouze features a dreamy woman in a low-cut, bejewelled gown. The lush background is pure Art Deco.*

*Far left: A stencil by George Barbier from the almanac* Guirlande des Mois, *1919.*

## FASHION ACCESSORIES

Other popular Art Deco fashion accessories included fans, which ranged from the simple contemporary designs in paper (often featuring an advertisement on the reverse side) to delicate silk and satin fantasies on carved wooden frames. The mother-of-pearl fans of the Frenchman Georges Bastard were among the most lavish accessories of the time, their delicate ribs patterned with stylised flowers, triangles or other geometric shapes. Bastard also designed boxes, bowls, lanterns and a wide range of jewels – bangles, hat pins, haircombs – in mother of pearl, ivory, jade, tortoiseshell, horn, rock crystal and coral.

Handbags were usually quite small, either in a 'clutch' style or with handles. They were sometimes covered with elaborate beading that was suspended from jewel-encrusted, silver, gold or platinum frames, or perhaps made of such exotic skins as lizard-, snake- or shark-skin (shagreen), and had gold or platinum clasps. Gemstones, accented with faceted or cabochon rubies, emeralds and sapphires and diamonds studded the frames. Semi-precious stones carved with Egyptian- and Oriental-inspired motifs were used for the clasps.

## HANDBAG MATERIALS

In the United States, steel mesh bags appeared, their metal frames frequently decorated with geometric designs in colourful enamels, or else studded with the cut-steel 'jewels' known as marcasites (these were also popular diamond substitutes in cheap jewellery). Brocade, embroidered and tapestry bags were plentiful as well, adorned with jazzy, geometrical designs or colourful floral patterns. An evening bag designed by Van Cleef & Arpels was embroidered with sequins sewn onto the fabric. Mauboussin designed elaborate evening bags with diamond and emerald clasps that matched the brooches and bracelets worn on the bearer's evening gown. By the late 1930s plastic was emerging as a stylish material, and bulky handbags – often round or rectangular – began to be carried, sometimes even by women of taste.

The top designers of the day included Paul Poiret; Elsa Schiaparelli, who at times courted the ludicrous inventions of the Surrealist artists and, among her many classic costumes,

*Above: A stylishly dressed couple poses on a paper fan, which would have been an advertising give-away.*

*Right: 'The Polo Game', a fashion plate dating from 1923. The woman's accessories – her hat, gloves and parasol – reflect the Art Deco love of colour.*

wittily designed a hat topped by a shoe, and a gown shaped like a lobster; Coco Chanel; Jean Patou; Madeleine Vionnet (who invented the bias cut); Jeanne Lanvin; Worth; Nina Ricci; Paquin; Christian Berard; Lucien Lelong; Jacques Doucet; and Mainbocher. Coco Chanel revolutionised haute couture with her chic daytime designs, including the classic short and tailored two-piece suit.

### ORPHIST FASHION

Some of the more jokey and humorous contributions to the Paris fashion scene were made by Sonia Delaunay, whose designs – like her brightly checked or zigzagged coats, dresses and hats – were influenced by the geometric elements of fine art. Her Orphist car was decorated in checks of bright colour; the matching coats, hats and interior were impressive adaptations of her husband's serious high art.

They reflected the heady *joie de vivre* of the Art Deco style.

### FASHION OUTSIDE FRANCE

Delaunay was quite serious about the whole enterprise: it was hard work creating fun; it was spirited, uplifting work. Her Orphist car, in particular, captured all the contradictions of Art Deco by means of one energetic leap into the machinery of the modern world. It was a remarkable feat of far-sightedness. Many of Delaunay's creations were quite similar to the avant-garde designs by the Russians Stepanova and Popova, with their practical lines and severe cuts quite removed from the heavily ornamented, exotic costumes of Poiret.

The contributions of other European countries and the United States were mostly pale reflections of what Paris was offering. Russia was deadly serious about the use of clothes

*Above: 'The Sweet Night', a fashion plate from the* Gazette du Bon Ton, *1920, features clothes designed by Worth.*

*Far left: Being geometric, the Greek key design on the frame of this French handbag fits nicely into Art Deco repertory.*

*Left: A detail of a smart clutch bag. The buckle is dotted with marcasites, which were popular imitation gems at the time.*

design in relation to the ordinary people, as it was in ceramic design, but it was not any less inventive for that. Again, artists like Tatlin and Rodchenko applied themselves to the design of clothes fit for the average working Russian. The results were not elegant, but the stark frugality of the cut and material would have looked completely in place in any pavilion dedicated to *L'Esprit Nouveau*.

## THE POPULARISATION OF FASHION

Yet while the story of fashion during the 1920s and 1930s has often been represented as being exclusively that of the major couture houses located in Paris, the names of Schiaparelli, Paquin, Worth, Chanel and Balenciaga represent but one facet of what amounted to a growing obsession among the women and, to a lesser extent, the men of the world.

## A UNIVERSAL STYLE

Far from being an upper-class domain, the new and stylish fashion was seen to percolate through every social rank in terms of clothing, hair and various accessories. Furthermore, the fashion of the upper – as well as of the middle and lower – classes was to a certain and unprecedented extent affected by the dress and appearance of the newly created, larger-than-life film stars. For perhaps the first time, originality and novelty in fashion came from more than one source and what was fashionable and accepted as such could just as well originate from Hollywood – say, from the smart geometric haircut sported by Louise Brooks, or the sexy pyjama suits of Marlene Dietrich – as from the French fashion journals. What is difficult to determine is where the impetus for actual change in fashion came from, and whether the stars of stage and screen were a reflection of, or a model for, popular taste.

The answer is that they were probably a combination of both, but what was immeasurably significant was the way in which style was disseminated to a huge audience.

In addition to films, the growth of the women's magazine industry, particularly in the United States, provided an information outlet and a stimulation for demand. *Vogue, The Queen* and *Harper's Bazaar* all contributed to a fashion consciousness which, until the late 1920s at least, the ordinary woman had been aware of, but as something beyond her own sphere of experience. Now, for many more women than before, there existed the opportunity to be

*Left: 'The Seaside', a fashion plate from* Art, Goût, Beauté, *1921, featuring designs by Molyneux, Beer, Doucet and Jenny.*

*Below: Film stars like Joan Crawford influenced what ordinary women wore.*

'fashionable' in a way which was truly a part of the swiftly changing modes and morals of the day. In short, the art of being fashionable was made easier by the fact that what was fashionable during the 1920s was so radically different from what had gone before.

The quest for contemporaneity could start with something as simple as a haircut: during the 1920s the bob, shingle, bingle or Eton crop. Hairstyles were always closely allied to other elements of prevailing fashion, and the reason for the shortness of the modern hairstyles during the 1920s may lie in the shift of the ever-changing focus on areas of the body as erogenous zones. Once again, the movies can be seen to play a role in this change in the public's taste. The vamp was born in silent American films of the early 1920s, best realised by the likes of Pola Negri and Theda Bara. Because of the nature of acting for soundless film, attention was focused on the eyes

*Le Cadran Solaire*

as tools of expression and dramatic effect. Kohl-rimmed orbs would glare in close-up from under exotic turbans or bandeaux pulled down over the brow, further accentuating the glowering, submissive, terrified or lustful stare of the ruby-red-lipped leading lady. It is no great leap to make between the look of the vamp smouldering under her turban, bandeau or close-fitting hat and the popularity of the face-framing cloche hat which endured for most of the 1920s.

## RISING HEMLINES

As we have seen, perhaps the most dramatic change in women's clothing was in the length of hemlines, which had been modestly low at the beginning of the 1920s but then shortened as the decade progressed. By 1925 the hemline had risen from the ankle to the knee, and once more the shifting erogenous zone was in evidence as the long-hidden female leg came boldly into view. What is more, it made its appearance clad in stockings, which were very often of flesh-coloured silk or the newer, excitingly modern (and not to mention cheaper) rayon. This material was also used for underwear and evening dresses, and between 1920 and 1925 its production rose from 8 million lbs to 53 million lbs in the United States alone.

## THE EMANCIPATED WOMAN

The shortening hemline can be allied, albeit tenuously, to the increasing emancipation of females, relating to both their consciousness and behaviour. Newly fashionable dresses were related to the acceptance of jazz music in certain circles and the ability to move to the music was of paramount importance. The reign of

*Left: A fashion plate by George Barbier for the 1921 'Le Cadran Solaire'.*

types of dress which were restrictive in this way therefore came swiftly to an end, for the young and fashionable realised that it was impossible to do the new dance called the 'Charleston' in a hobble skirt or the 'Black Bottom' in a whalebone corset.

### THE CHANGING SILHOUETTE

Although the silhouette of the fashionable female was not subject to all of the rigours it had experienced in the previous century, body shape was still conditioned by the restrictive foundation garment called the 'flattener'. This was a device worn over the bust literally to flatten the profile of the woman, thus giving her a boyish physique commensurate with the fashionable boyish hairstyles. This in turn allowed for the 'tube dress' to take precedence, a dress whose look paid no heed to the 'ins and outs' of the female body. There was also the mass acceptance of the fashionable 'jumper'. First sold around 1922, the jumper was to form an integral part of the young woman's wardrobe. Generally, it was worn pulled down around the hips with a blouse underneath and a short pleated skirt. In terms of everyday fashion, this look was to endure to the end of the decade, and it is important, too, because it was a look transcending the boundaries of class.

### BLURRING CLASS BOUNDARIES

The difference between mass fashion and couture, though, was realised through the types and qualities of materials used. The luxury of evening dresses and the social life that demanded them were, of course, the realm of high fashion and the rich, the glittering arena

*Right: The front page of a 1920 issue of* Le Rire *features a flapper versus a feminist.*

No 96. – 4 Décembre 1920.
26e ANNÉE

France et Colonies  Étranger
Trois mois... 9.50  10. »
Six mois..... 18. »  19.50
Un an........ 35. »  38. »

Les abonnements partent du 1er de chaque mois.

# Le Rire

JOURNAL HUMORISTIQUE PARAISSANT LE SAMEDI

75 Centimes

F. JUVEN, éditeur
1, rue de Choiseul, 1
PARIS

Tout changement d'adresse doit être accompagné de 50 centimes.

Copyright 1920 by LE RIRE, Paris

TOTOTE EST CONSERVATRICE

— Moi, ma petite, je suis féministe.
— Eh bien! pas moi : j'aime mieux les hommes.

Dessin de F. FABIANO.

*Above: This fashion plate appeared in* Art, Goût, Beauté *in 1921. The slim line of the dress, its high neck and the elaborate, plumed hat were common features of the haute couture of the 1920s.*

in which the names of Chanel, Schiaparelli, Balenciaga and their other haute-couture contemporaries came into their own. For although some of their designs would eventually affect the contents of the ordinary working girl's wardrobe, their most immediate sphere of influence extended into the *beau monde*, of which they were a distinct part. Indeed, Schiaparelli was renowned for her concept of introducing styles inspired by honest working clothes into high society, once more shifting the impetus for change in clothing fashion.

### THE STYLE OF THE 1930S

The beginning of the 1930s saw a turnaround by the leaders of fashion, who sought to lengthen the skirts which had reached their zenith of shortness at the peak of the jazz age. Perhaps it was the effects of the great slump, but the 1930s witnessed a dissolution of a single style for fashionable women and the embracing of many different styles, both in Europe and North America. Short hair and the cloche hat lost their supreme position and were replaced by longer, wavy locks and the small hat perched rakishly on the side of the head. This new style was accompanied by the lengthening of skirts until the hems were on average 10 in (25 cm) above the ground.

### THE RETURN OF THE WAIST

The one concession to fashion which every woman was to make, regardless of the style or detailing of the rest of her dress, was in the waist. The return of the boned corset was only interrupted by the demands on both bodies and materials occasioned by the outbreak of World War II. The small waist was, more often than not, complemented by an exaggeration in the width of the shoulders, a look in part prompted by Joan Crawford.

In the realms of haute couture and evening wear the area of emphasis shifted once again and the back came into its own. Indeed, even some day wear was slit at the back to show bare skin. This trend grew along with the general public passion for sport and sportswomen, which was especially strong during the 1930s. In swimming and tennis, for instance, the clothes worn by both the professionals and amateurs became much more practical and, because of this, much more revealing. The growth of golf as a game for both men and women also meant that fashionable ladies were seen attired in practical and clothing on the links. The growth of sunbathing and the belief in the beneficial effects of a suntan – as well as its social cachet – also meant that flesh had to be revealed rather than concealed.

*Above: The actress Marlene Dietrich dressed in the height of fashion.*

*Left: This stained-glass window by Jacques Gruber reflects the golfing craze.*

## MEN'S FASHIONS

In terms of men's clothing, cut had resolved itself by the mid-1920s and the greatest changes to occur were in the choice of materials. The suit continued to be a staple of the average man's wardrobe, but there was a distinct and growing move towards the casual, which continued through the 1920s and into the 1930s. Notwithstanding the elegance of the upper-class male in top hat and tails, personified by Fred Astaire, the everyday man was seen in the lounge suit, which changed only in small details. By the mid-1920s, the waistcoat had fallen out of favour, prompting the move to the double-breasted coat. By the end of the decade, however, the waistcoat was back in fashion, worn as a double-breasted garment under a single-breasted coat.

## MEN'S TROUSERS

By far the most outrageous change in the cut of men's clothing between the wars was in the width of the trousers. The 'Oxford Bag', so called because the style was originated and adopted by the undergraduates of Oxford University, gained rapid popularity, but this had diminished by the end of the 1920s. Yet the width of the trouser leg was still to remain relatively wide until the end of the 1930s. Other menswear novelties included plus fours (short trousers for shooting which were adopted for golfing and then for town wear), the motoring cap, the boater and the blazer. All these were peripheral developments however-er, and were set against the changing backdrop of social and economic upheaval which characterised these fashion-fixated years.

*Below left: a jaunty caricature of the French performer Maurice Chevalier, sporting a straw boater and suntan.*

*Below: a pencil and gouache fashion illustration by Ernest Deutsch Dryden.*

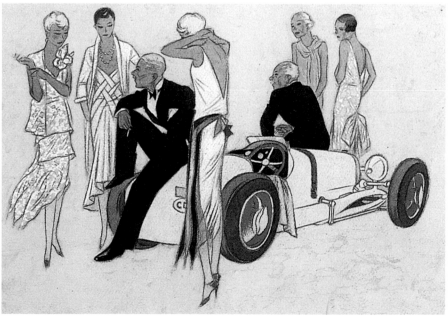

# ART DECO
# JEWELLERY AND FASHION
# ACCESSORIES

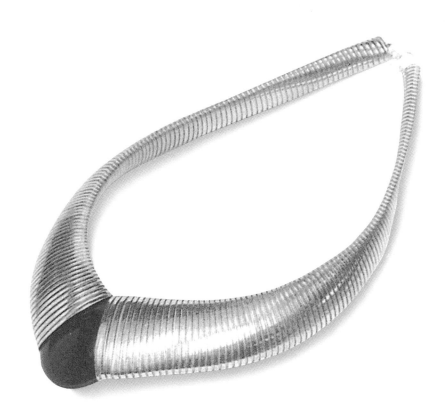

**J**ewellery is often regarded as a trivial luxury, a little extra touch that sets off an article of clothing. Apart from the wonderful creations by Jean Puiforcat in the area of tableware, it is in the field of jewellery that Art Deco reaches the zenith of its stylishness. If the designs for furniture or building interiors sometimes looked clumsy or not quite right, the intimate scale of jewellery could disguise those shortcomings. Indeed, jewellery is one of the most exciting disciplines of the 1920–30 era.

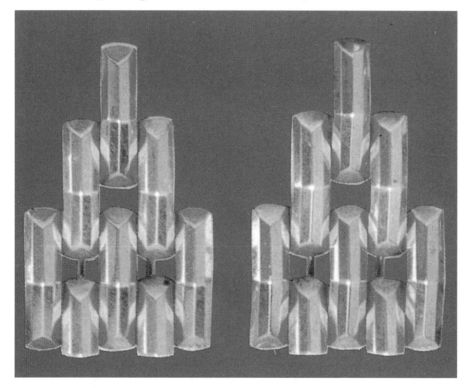

*Preceding page: this chrome necklace is strikingly set off by pieces of bright synthetic plastic. The chain is intricately fashioned, solid yet flexible, and easily worn.*

*Above: the outstanding manifestation of Art Deco in the United States was its architecture. Some architectonic jewellery was inspired by skyscrapers, and these stepped gold clips are by Tiffany & Co.*

The jewellers of the Art Deco period produced some of the most dazzling pieces ever seen – daring, pristine and even playful. Unlike the Art Nouveau and Arts and Crafts periods, when noted designers held prime positions and had a strong influence on other individuals, the Art Deco years were strong on design itself; many quintessential pieces were anonymously designed, unsigned (except perhaps for a jeweller's mark), and indeed of uncertain national origin. So wide-ranging and pervasive a style was Art Deco that similar pieces – necklaces of, say, Bakelite and chrome – were being manufactured in places as disparate as New Jersey and Czechoslovakia.

### THE GEOMETRIC INFLUENCE
While the Art Nouveau movement freed jewellery design from the antiquated influences of the nineteenth century, Art Deco took this evolution a step further, introducing geometrical forms and brilliant colour schemes. Unlike Art Nouveau jewellery, which often involved realistic floral, figural or faunal motifs, Art Deco was simpler; it was usually either geometric or abstract, and even when it featured flowers or other realistic elements these were quite subtle and underplayed.

### FREEDOM OF EXPRESSION
The jewellery and accessories of the Art Deco period were as varied and colourful as the fashions themselves. The great French goldsmiths created miniature works of art in platinum, gold, diamonds, emeralds and other precious gems – some starkly geometric, others with Egyptian or Oriental overtones, still others wildly floral and encrusted with stones of many colours. Such hard stones as onyx, turquoise, jade and lapis lazuli were also used, and enamelling was widely applied.

The myriad influences contributing to Art Deco jewellery came from pharoanic Egypt, the Orient, tribal Africa, from machines and graphic design, even from buildings, such as stepped Mayan temples and their latter-day descendants, the big-city skyscrapers. The abstract qualities of Art Deco jewellery can be traced to some of various avant-garde art movements that arose during the first decade of the twentieth century.

### THE INFLUENCE OF ART

Picasso's *Demoiselles d'Avignon,* painted in 1907, launched the Cubist movement in its division of the human figure into flat, overlapping, geometric configurations. In 1909 the Italian poet Marinetti published the *Futurist Manifesto*, which heralded the machine, urban life and speed as the pictorial expression of a new reality. The Dutch De Stijl painter Piet Mondrian took Cubism a step further, into neoplasticism. Through abstraction, he freed forms from any suggestion of objective reality.

As early as 1913, many of these new artistic concepts were evident in jewellery design, particularly in France. In the United States, where modernism in jewellery design was resisted fiercely for many years, a critic for the *Jewelers' Circular Weekly* (of 26 March 1913) asked, 'Will the new movement in painting and sculpture be reflected in the forthcoming jewelry?' The article went on to conclude, concerning Cubism and Futurism, that 'whether the exhibits appeal to us or not the vital impulse toward something new and simple is apparent on every hand'.

### ART DECO MOTIFS

The principle motifs in Art Deco jewellery design were simple geometric forms, such as the square, circle, rectangle and triangle. These

*Above: an intricately fashioned essay in geometry, this 1930s' gilded-metal necklace has a strong machine-age feel. The piece is French, but its maker is unknown.*

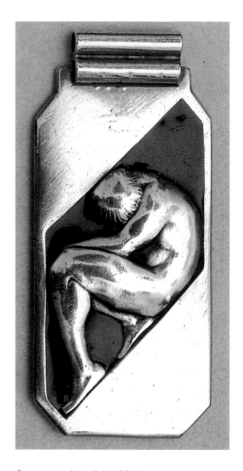

*Above: An Arcadian pipe-player occupies a roundel of pavé-set diamonds in this brooch by Boucheron dating from c.1910.*

*Right: A handsome enamelled-silver pendant made by French jeweller Emile Davide during the 1920s.*

shapes were often juxtaposed or overlapped to create complex linear configurations. Abstract patterns, derived from the architecture of ancient civilisations, such as Babylonian ziggurats and stepped Mayan and Aztec temples, also found their way into the contours of jewellery design. Although images of animals of speed and grace – the greyhound, the gazelle and the deer – as well as of the new-fangled automobiles and aeroplanes were found on both precious and mass-produced

jewels, human subjects were not as common as on Art Nouveau goldsmiths' work, but some noted designers depicted them in their creations, and, more often, they appeared on inexpensive, anonymous baubles.

## CLASSICAL INSPIRATION
René Lalique moulded some of his pendants on romantic women; stylised African heads formed brooches by Chanel and others; Emile Davide favoured handsome, neo-classical

figures; and stylish 1920s' women were cut from cheap white metals, sometimes attached by tiny chains to modish canines.

Sir Flinders Petrie's archaeological excavations during the first decade of the century started an Egyptian craze. Howard Carter's discovery of Tutankhamen's tomb in 1922, and the press coverage that this generated for ten years, ensured a continuing interest in Egyptian art. The clean lines of hieroglyphic calligraphy reiterated the linear concepts that had begun to emerge before the war. Van Cleef & Arpels, among others, introduced stylised pharoanic motifs into their series of bracelets, shoulder clips and brooches. Diamonds, rubies, emeralds and sapphires were interchanged with such neutral stones as onyx.

## GEMS AND METALS

The materials used by the Art Deco jewellery-makers ranged from the traditional and precious to the unorthodox and innovative, like plastic, chrome and steel. Art Deco jewellery incorporated gold and silver, and precious and semi-precious stones, in designs that emphasised their contrasting colourative effects. Strong, earthy and unrefined colours dominated. Semi-precious stones, such as amber, jade, lapis lazuli, coral, turquoise, topaz, tourmaline, onyx, amethyst, aquamarine and rock crystal (some of which had been incorporated into Art Nouveau jewellery) gave jewellery settings vibrancy and interest, especially when placed next to such precious stones as diamonds (mostly baguette cut) and emeralds. Faceted and flat stones provided additional contrast in their different surface treatments.

As with furniture, the use of exotic new stones and metals was promoted. No longer limited to the traditional precious stones and metals, the jewellery designers made full use of new materials. Until 1900, stones were set almost exclusively in gold and sterling silver, often to the visual detriment of a piece of jewellery. The discovery of platinum as a setting in the first decade of the twentieth century, and its perfection a few years later – it was used in the manufacture of explosives during World War I – and adoption as a setting meant that the other elements could be accentuated. Platinum is a far stronger metal than gold or silver, which allows a stone to be set with very little supporting mounting. The settings for stones could therefore be reduced to just two or three retaining teeth. Art Deco jewellery therefore became both lighter in weight and more delicate in appearance. Van Cleef & Arpels developed the *serti invisible* (invisible setting), in which several rows of stones are placed next to each other with no apparent mounting. Although this technique was not perfected until 1935, a few pieces of the firm's jewellery from the early 1920s have survived to show its initial experiments.

## MODERN MATERIALS

Other new materials used were onyx, ebony, chrome, plastic, lapis lazuli, lacquered metals, agate, coral, Bakelite, rhinestones, jade, tortoiseshell, jet and moonstone. Used in conjunction, these materials offered up a riot of colour and contrasting textures. The types of jewellery and accessories produced were as

*Below: This diamond, ruby, emerald and sapphire bracelet by Lacloche Frères exemplifies the Egyptian-revival aspect of Art Deco.*

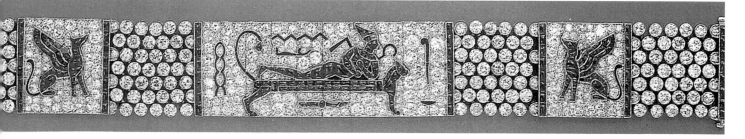

*Left: A white-gold brooch, probably French, set with emeralds, rubies, diamonds and moonstones.*

*Below: A silver, malachite and sodalite brooch made in the 1930s by Jean Desprès.*

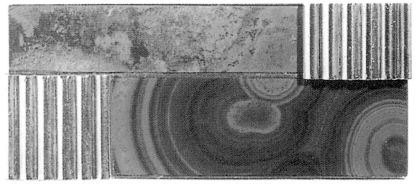

varied as the materials available: cigarette holders, rings, geometric necklaces, diamond and jet pins, glass pendants and wristwatches for day and evening wear. It was the pearl, however, that became a dominant gem of the period. During the nineteenth century, Oriental pearls had been treasured because of their scarcity. George Gould, son of the railway magnate Jay Gould, is reputed to have spent $500,000 on a string of pearls as a gift for his wife. After Mikimoto developed a technique for producing cultured pearls in Japan, however, pearls were available to a wider market. They could be set with other stones, worn in chokers around the neck, or in single strands, and became the accepted accessories for any occasion. A testimony to the popularity of pearls during the 1920s is evidenced by the following quotation from *Vogue* magazine: 'Day after day, I used to see poor Regina frying in that Lido in torture getting her neck brown. She did it, of course, for her pearls'.

By 1929 the jeweller's abstract creations had evolved into mechanistic forms based on industrial design. Indeed, the modern design principles inherent in automobile and aeroplane construction inspired a new decorative vocabulary for jewellery. Jewellery design had evolved from the thin, delicate creations of the early 1920s into bolder, larger designs with sharp outlines. The rainbow palette of bright colours gave way to muted tones. Stark contrast was achieved with black and white, epitomised by onyx and diamonds. Indeed, the diamond reigned supreme, cut in the new baguette style and placed next to other stones for contrast. There was also a return to the coloured diamond.

## FASHION'S INFLUENCE

Although many of the changes that took place

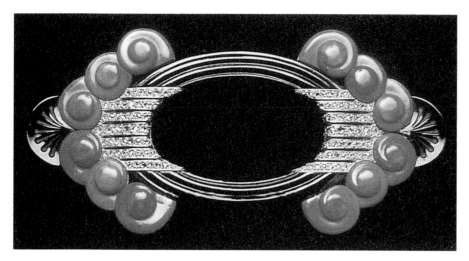

*Below: A pair of emerald and diamond earrings by Van Cleef & Arpels.*

in the field of jewellery design during the 1920s and 1930s occurred primarily for artistic reasons, fashion also directly influenced the style, size and shape of Art Deco jewellery. The introduction of rayon and muslin – materials too light to bear the weight of a heavy piece of jewellery – necessitated lighter pieces, now made possible with platinum. The new style in women's clothing – cloche hats, short hair, short hemlines, short sleeves – had furthermore changed the type of jewellery that was required to set the look off, and demanded complementary forms and types. The new look necessitated new jewellery with simple lines, minimum design and vivid colours.

### NECKLACES

Sleeveless, low-cut dresses accentuated the two main areas where jewels could be worn: the neck and the wrists. To accentuate the vertical line of the tubular dress, jewellery designers introduced long, dangling necklaces influenced by the multi-stranded models of the Indian maharajahs. Women wore such *sautoirs* and strings of beads in materials such as ivory, wood and semi-precious stones, either in the traditional manner or hanging down the back, over one shoulder, or even wrapped round one leg. Necklaces, suspended with pendants and tassels, hung as far as the stomach or, on occasion, even to the knees. In the dance-crazy 'Roaring Twenties', long necklaces complemented the short tunic dresses, fast dances and swaying movements.

### BROOCHES

The simple dresses, in contrast to the turn-of-the-century styles, and the simple hats could be decorated with small brooches (pins) and clasps. Brooches were worn attached to hats, shoulders, straps or belts. Perhaps the most important single innovation was the invention of the double-sided clip or clasp. The clips could be used in pairs to hold material together, or separately as brooches and pins. Such versatile, multiple-use jewellery (pieces comprising two or more components which could be dismantled and used separately) became

*Right: Georges Fouquet fashioned this gold brooch. Many of his pieces displayed a machine-age sensibility*

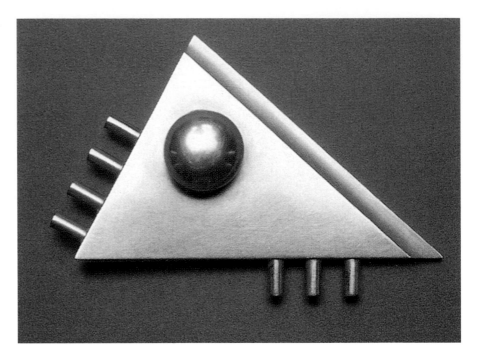

popular after the crash of 1929 and during the subsequent Depression. Pendants could double as brooches or be attached to lapels. The double barrette, formed from two linked pins, could be separated and worn in two places. The finest pieces came from the major jewellery houses, but they were imitated in less expensive materials for the mass market.

### BROOCH-BUCKLES

At the cheaper end of the scale, hundreds of different designs were brought out for buttons used on everyday wear. The brooch-buckle was composed of a ring of onyx, crystal or coral, either in a circle or an ellipse, with decorative motifs at either end using diamonds, pearls or sapphires. Black, Starr & Frost advertised a typical example in 1926 set with oxblood coral, diamonds and onyx. The brooch-buckle and the pin – another piece of jewellery which became popular during this period – could be worn either on a belt or attached to the cloche, the hat which sat securely on the wearers' heads over their fashionably cropped, shingled or bobbed hair.

### EARRINGS AND BANDEAUX

Such short hairstyles not only did away with the demand for elaborate extras like combs, but also exposed the ear for the first time, and long, dangling earrings of diamond, jade, ivory, jet, onyx, crystal and amber became fashionable, while small ear clips also appeared in myriad handsome guises. By 1929 earrings were so long that they touched the shoulder, further emphasising the verticality of fashion.

In response to the new, slender fashions at the beginning of the century, the bandeau had replaced the tiara and diadem. Still desired as an ornament worn in the evening, women in the 1920s wore the bandeau on the hairline, or set back on the head, like a halo.

In 1930 the French jeweller Chaumet designed an elegant diamond bandeau with three rosettes and stylised foliage. While in the United States, Oscar Heyman & Bros, a jeweller's jeweller which still manufactures fine jewellery for other prestigious firms, designed a delicate, diamond-studded example.

Because the typical Art Deco dress was sleeveless, it allowed the jewellery designer free rein to design creative jewellery with which to decorate the wrists and upper arm. There were several types of bracelets. The first

*Above: A red and black piece of jewellery by Boucheron, c.1925.*

*Left: A simple rock-crystal, platinum and diamond pendant necklace created by Georges Fouquet in 1924.*

*Above: A pair of jade, onyx and diamond earrings fashioned by Boucheron of Paris.*

*Above right: A diamond, aquamarine and giant-citrine pendant brooch made by the Parisian firm Maison Mellerrio.*

were flat, flexible, narrow bands decorated with stylised designs of flowers, geometricised shapes and motifs from Egypt and Persia. Because these were narrow, four or five were worn together on the wrist. Toward the end of the 1920s they became wider. Big, square links of coral, rock crystal, onyx and *pavé* diamonds were accentuated with emeralds, rubies, sapphires and other cabochon-cut gems. Other types, bangles or slave bracelets, were worn on the upper arm or just above the elbow. They were made out of gold, silver and materials such as bamboo. Like the flexible bracelets, several were worn at a time.

**EVENING BRACELETS**

Artist-jewellers like Jean Fouquet, Raymond Templier, Jean Desprès and Gérard Sandoz combined a variety of stones and metals. In Sweden, Wiwen Nilsson mixed silver with large pieces of crystal. A third type, worn in the evening, consisted of loose strands of pearls held together by a large, pearl-studded medallion from which additional strings of pearls were suspended. Like the bangle, it was worn above the elbow. A vogue that was to have little effect on the top-class jewellers was the wearing of heavy, primitive bangles, although Jean Fouquet was one of the few to exploit the fashion with African-style bracelets.

With sleeveless dresses and the rage for sports, the watch bracelet became very popular during the 1920s. Jean Patou introduced the *garçonne*-type (the boyish woman) into fashion when he outfitted the tennis star Suzanne Lenglen. Every woman wanted to look the part of the sportswoman, even if she did not participate.

**WRISTWATCHES**

Cartier is credited with designing the world's first wristwatch, as well as what some consider the most significant wristwatch ever made: the 'Tank' watch. The wristwatch, worn during the day, was plain and strapped with leather or ribbon. The evening watch resembled a richly jewelled bracelet set with pearls and diamonds, either enameled or made of different colours of gold. An example from the period by Tiffany & Co was set with diamonds and onyx and mounted in platinum. Between 1925 and 1930 the pendant and châteleine watches became popular. Suspended from a

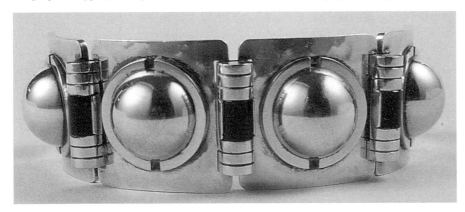

*Left: This gilt-silver and onyx articulated bracelet is by Jean Desprès, 1930.*

*Below: a 1930s' multi-linked bracelet made of enamelled and silvered white metal.*

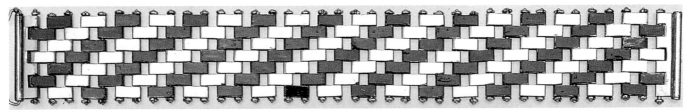

*Below: The firm of Louis Cartier fashioned this pendant watch of diamonds, jade, onyx and sapphires (shown front and back).*

ribbon or silk cord, the face of the watch was upside down so that the wearer could glance downwards to determine the time. (An example by Van Cleef and Arpels shows its Eastern influence with its jade, enamelling and Oriental motifs; this pendant watch, suspended from a *sautoir* chain, was worn in the evening. The chain was studded with pearls, diamonds and coloured gems. Its case was also embellished with diamonds.)

After World War I, rings grew far larger and bolder, dominating the finger. Surfaces were smooth, polished or satinised metals. Stones could be either precious or semi-precious, set with pavé diamonds or a combination of two lacquered metals.

Towards the end of the 1920s, when gloves went out of fashion and muffs were preferred for the new, fur-trimmed coats, women began to wear massive rings to adorn their now

*Above: A cocktail watch by Paul-Emile Brandt, its platinum bracelet highlighted with diamonds and emeralds.*

*Far left and left: Three tiny rhinestone and paste timepieces, with Swiss-made works and elaborate frames. They could be worn as brooches or pendants.*

gloveless hands. The popularity of the fan as an accessory for evening wear gave them a further opportunity to show off the latest in ring fashions. Suzanne Belperron's large ring in carved chalcedony, set with a single Oriental pearl, captured the new mood.

## VARIED INSPIRATIONS

Other ring designers offered widely different solutions. Jean Desprès combined crystal, gold and silver to make abstract geometric patterns influenced by Cubism and African masks; Fritz Schwerdt, working in Germany, designed rings that were inspired by machines, one of which reproduced precisely the inner mechanism of a rotary engine in which an agate rod acted as the connecting pin.

## MEN'S JEWELLERY

The Art Deco style was also reflected in men's jewellery, although never with the same flair as women's. Geometric forms characterised the dials of men's pocket watches, which were mounted in platinum set with onyx, diamonds,

pearls, emeralds, rubies and topazes. Watch chains were made up of cylinder links enhanced with polished or faceted stones. Cufflinks followed the same general shapes. Jean Fouquet designed a notable pair with enamelled Cubist motifs; Black, Starr & Frost's selection included a pair made of onyx with diamond borders.

### BEJEWELLED FASHION ACCESSORIES
Fashion accessories – vanity cases, handbags, powder compacts, fans, cigarette cases – were designed in abundance during the 1920s and 1930s, often with bold geometric and floral motifs that were every bit as masterful as those decorating furniture, ceramics and textiles. Mauboussin, Lacloche Frères, Fouquet, Marchak, Mellerio, Tiffany & Co, Boucheron, Cartier, Chaumet and Van Cleef & Arpels were some of the major jewellers whose output included not only standard jewellery items but also fashion accessories for the well-dressed lady of the period and an amazing variety of *objets d'art*, some of which are really more jewellery than object, with elements carved in semi-precious stones set in silver and gold and often elaborately lacquered. Influenced by Chinese, Japanese, Persian and medieval art, these *objets d'art* combined coloured gemstones, precious stones, marcasite, enamel and lacquer. The small cigarette cases designed by Gérard Sandoz introduced a further type of decoration in their use of crushed *coquille d'oeuf* (eggshell). Whether it was a vanity or cigarette case, compact, lighter, lipstick case, mirror or handbag, each item was intended as a miniature work of art.

*Left: Casino de Paris performer Mistinguett flaunts her elaborate ring and bracelets in this poster by Charles Gesmar, 1925.*

*Left: Van Cleef & Arpel's elaborate vanity case features a Japanese landscape of inlaid gold, abalone and mother of pearl.*

*Below left: This Van Cleef & Arpels vanity case is primarily of lapis lazuli, with a carved centre panel dotted with diamonds.*

### CARTIER'S *OBJETS D'ART*

By 1920, for example, Cartier's *oeuvre* included such luxury *objets* as vanity cases, jewel caskets, lighters and timepieces. Cartier's pieces were highly decorative, and often pictorial. He created vanity cases adorned with Chinese landscapes in mother of pearl, coloured enamels and rubies. The *nécessaire*, or vanity case, which held a mirror, compact, lipstick and comb, took its form from the Japanese *inro* (a small case divided into several compartments). Although small in size, it accommodated all of the accoutrements that a lady might need.

### NEW FORMS OF ACCESSORIES

Vanities were mostly rectangular or oval, and hung from a silk cord. In 1930 the vanity case was enlarged into the *minaudière* by Alfred Van Cleef, who named it this after witnessing his wife simper (*minauder*) into the mirror. The *minaudière* replaced the evening bag and daytime dress bag.

Powder compacts and cigarette cases became *de rigueur* during the 1920s for the bold woman of fashion, who could now smoke and powder her nose in public. Inexpensive versions of these items, as well as of vanity cases, also proliferated, especially in France and the United States. These were fashioned of paste, plastic and base metal, and the application of coloured enamel to the metal pieces often made them – despite being cheap and mass-produced – every bit as

handsome as the more expensive models. They were sometimes marked with the cosmetic firm's name – Richard Hudnut, Coty, Helena Rubenstein – but were more often engraved with such evocative words as Volupté or Zanadu. One Coty compact was covered all over with a René Lalique design of stylised powder puffs in black, orange, white and gold; the same design appeared on a cardboard powder box and has recently been in production again.

### THE USE OF INDUSTRIAL METAL
Firms who manufactured industrial metal, such as Elgin American in Illinois, diversified to produce compacts and vanity cases which were often superbly engineered in enamelled chrome or another white metal and which sold for a dollar or less. Many of the cheaper varieties of accessories sported either figural or faunal decorative designs – stylishly clad ladies, graceful deer or greyhounds, playful Scotties, for example. Enamelled cigarette cases for both men and women were covered with rich geometric, sunburst or zigzag patterns, or were often adorned with a stone stud or two.

*Above left: a black enamel compact set with diamonds by Cartier, c.1925.*

*Above: this compact and matching lipstick case by Elgin American is handsomely presented as a boxed set.*

# NOTED
# ART DECO
# JEWELLERS

*Left: A stunningly elegant Art Deco brooch by Georges Fouquet.*

*Preceding page: Pendant brooch and Coldstream brooch by Cartier (top left) and bracelet and brooch by Lacloche.*

The Swiss-born designer Jean Dunand, whose hammered-metal and lacquered vases, furniture and screens were greatly indebted to Asian and other non-Western styles, also designed a small but stunning body of jewellery. Largely of hammered silver lacquered with red and black, Dunand's dangling earrings and earclips, brooches and bracelets, assumed bold geometric shapes containing equally strong motifs – interwoven or superimposed lines, zigzags, openwork squares and triangles and so on. Their kinship with the painting of the time is immediately evident, and indeed Dunand often collaborated with Cubist painter and sculptor Jean Lambert-Ruckion on large projects. He produced a particularly striking pair of earrings with dangling black enamel grids which were reminiscent in style of the '*Gitterwerk*' of turn-of-the-century Vienna.

### FOUQUET *PÈRE ET FILS*

Georges and Jean Fouquet were father and son and both created outstanding jewels during the Art Deco period. Georges, who had also produced Art Nouveau goldsmith's work for La Maison Fouquet, tended towards busier designs, whereas Jean leaned to more geometric forms, *à la* Templier and Sandoz 'art jewels'. The firm also commissioned jewellery from Eric Bagge, the noted architect and interior designer; painter André Leveille; and the premier poster artist-illustrator of the day, A M Cassandre.

**P**aris, of course, was both the source and the trendsetter of Art Deco so it follows that it should have led the way in *moderne* jewellery, and many renowned French goldsmiths created lovely, often one-of-a-kind, jewels for their exclusive clientele.

*Left: Raymond Templier produced some of Art Deco's boldest geometric designs. The central panel of this silver bracelet, dating from 1925 to 1930, can also be worn as a brooch.*

*Below: A gold, onyx, enamel and diamond brooch by Gérard Sandoz, the Parisian jeweller, dating from 1928.*

## GÉRARD SANDOZ

Gérard Sandoz came from a family of jewellery-makers, and began to design stark, geometric pieces for the Sandoz firm while still in his teens. His goldsmith's *oeuvre* dates from a period of just under a decade, yet his output is nonetheless significant within the realm of Art Deco jewellery. The clean lines and delicate craftsmanship of Sandoz's undeniably machine-age pieces, with smooth, shiny or matt metal 'parts' featuring materials like onyx and coral, and punctuated by a single aquamarine 'stud' or a line of diamonds contributed to their significant place in the Art Deco repertoire. This work spanned only about a decade, for he later turned to film-making and painting.

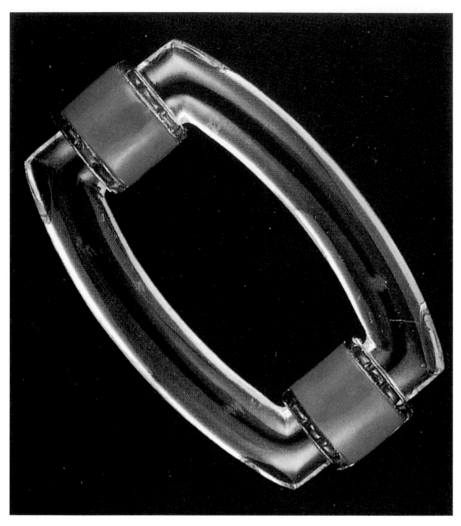

*Above: This rock crystal, coral, onyx and sapphire brooch by the Parisian firm of René Boivin is a lovely example of a sparsely geometric, subtly coloured jewel.*

## RAYMOND TEMPLIER

Raymond Templier, like Sandoz, came from a family of Parisian jewellers, Maison Templier having been started by his grandfather during the mid-nineteenth century. Templier's designs, like Deprès', were boldly geometric, but sported more precious stones, for instance brooches with scatterings of diamonds against stark platinum fields. Templier was especially fond of precious white metals – platinum and silver – and paired them with onyx and other dark stones in stunning pieces (these black-and-white colour combinations were wildly popular during the Art Deco period). His designs for the actress Brigitte Helm's jewels in the film *L'Argent* were marvellously theatrical, especially in the blatantly architectonic ear pendants which could be miniature Empire State buildings or John Storrs sculptures. Templier collaborated with the designer Michel Percheron and at least once with the Cubist sculptor-painter Gustave Miklos, whose delicate plaster model of an elongated head he translated into a brooch of white and yellow gold. A bracelet containing a brooch in the Virginia Museum of Fine Art's collection in Richmond, Virginia, is an outstanding example of his intricate designs: the wide, silver band centres on a removable brooch of platinum, white gold and diamonds, which is itself rectilinear but which features a large, round diamond.

Other noted Art Deco 'art jewellers', whose output was small but significant in terms of design, included Paul-Emile Brandt and René Boivin, whose firm produced its handsome *moderne* designs under the direction of Madame Boivin and her two daughters. Much more prolific, however, and in turn influential, were the mostly long-established jewellery firms producing *deluxe* pieces – Cartier,

Boucheron, Janesich, Chaumet, Mellerio, Fouquet, Vever and Van Cleef & Arpels.

## LOUIS CARTIER

The Cartier firm produced more traditional and less geometric jewels. Louis Cartier (1875–1942) was the third generation of his family to head the House of Cartier in Paris, which had been founded by his grandfather in 1847. Cartier was fascinated by the Ballets Russes, and was also influenced by the arts of Egypt, the Islamic world and the Orient, as well as by the craftsmanship of the legendary Peter Carl Fabergé, goldsmith to the Russian imperial family.

## ORIENTAL INFLUENCES

The year 1910 was a significant one for Cartier: upon viewing the Ballets Russes' production of *Scheherezade*, he and his assistant Charles Jacqueau altered not only the firm's palette but also the types of gems they used. The colours and designs of Cartier's jewels became quite daring and innovative, as did the actual composition of the pieces, which now featured both precious and semi-precious gems in dramatic settings. Geometric patterns appeared, but when compared with the bold, stark designs of Templier, Sandoz and others, Cartier's jewels were extremely decorative, even pictorial: his diamond brooches, for example, taking the form of overflowing flower baskets, while also common to his repertory were elaborate figural motifs inspired by the exotic worlds of India, Egypt and the Middle and Far East.

*Right: A stunning cigarette case by Cartier, worked in mother of pearl, coral and diamonds. Note especially the turtle with its red shell.*

*Above: A diamond and platinum cornucopia brooch by an unknown French maker.*

*Right: A winged scarab brooch by Cartier, 1924. The body is of smoked quartz, the wings of faience and emeralds.*

## EXOTIC INSPIRATION

Cartier's fascination with exotic motifs led to the creation of diamond, ruby and platinum earrings from which hung jade roundels carved with elephants, and a gold and enamel bangle with two carved-stone chimera heads facing each other in the centre.

## FIGURAL MOTIFS

During the 1930s, figural clips and brooches, featuring ornate 'blackamoor' heads, and even Native American squaws and chiefs, were marketed by Cartier and spawned a whole wave of cheap imitations, especially in plastics and base metals. A great deal of carved jade and coral was used in Cartier's rings, brooches, jabot pins, bracelets and necklaces, and motifs such as heavily bejewelled baskets or swags of flowers, berries and fruit (popularly known as 'fruit salads' or 'tutti frutti') were composed of rich, colourful masses of carved emeralds, rubies and sapphires amid variously cut and set diamonds. Jewellers also engraved emeralds, jade, coral and lapis lazuli in imitation of Oriental jewellery (the stones were often carved in the Orient and shipped to the West for setting).

## THE CHANGING STYLE

Cartier, Black, Starr & Frost, J E Caldwell and Co and Van Cleef & Arpels mixed engraved stones in figurative compositions, such as animals and baskets of fruit and flowers, that took their inspiration from Japanese and Egyptian prototypes. Such motifs worked their way into the ever-growing repertoire of costume jewellery too, with French, American, Czechoslovakian and other factories flooding the market with paste resembling diamonds, rubies, emeralds, onyx and jade. By the end of the 1920s, jewellers refined gem-cutting

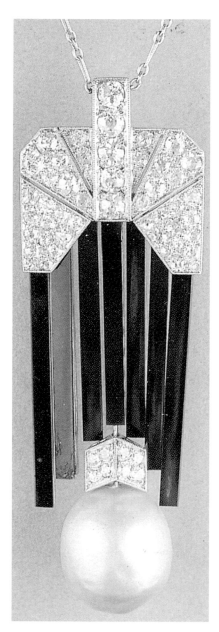

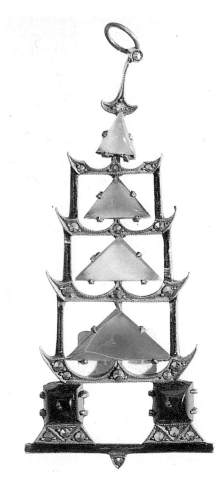

*Left: A pendant by Lacloche Frères fashioned from platinum, diamonds, onyx and pearl.*

*Below: A pendant shaped in the form of a pagoda by the German firm Theodor Fahrner.*

further by the introduction of several new shapes, such as the baguette, trapezium, table and square cut.

## GLASS JEWELLERY

The glass jewellery of René Lalique – the undisputed *maître verrier* (master of glass) – and Gabriel Argy-Rousseau deserves special mention. By the 1920s Lalique was creating some spectacular glass jewellery, including round and oval medallions moulded with female figures, insects and flowers, some in bright hues, others in subtly stained frosted glass. He also created all-glass rings, moulded with tiny flowers; expandable bracelets of wide rectangular sections decorated with stylised organic designs; necklaces made up partly or wholly of hemispherical, zigzag, floral, foliate or round beads; and brooches and buckles backed by coloured foil and metal depicting subjects as varied as moths, a satyr, serpents and a grazing stag. His pendants, some inspired by open-work Japanese swordguards, or *tsubas*, and moulded with stylised leaf or animal designs, others with insects and beautiful female figures, all hung from silk cords terminating in rich tassels.

## GABRIEL ARGY-ROUSSEAU

*Pâte-de-verre* master Argy-Rousseau also produced jewellery: one diamond-shaped pendant features a white elephant in a leafy surround; a round medallion depicts a curtsying ballerina amid a floral border; and a further pendant – this one oval – has three scarab beetles, one of many Egyptian motifs made popular during the 1920s.

*Left: Sybil Dunlop created this long 1930s necklace, with a tassel pendant and matching clips of silver and chrysoprase.*

Among other well-known *deluxe* designers, Mauboussin was noted for his highly colourful pieces, often set in black enamel; Boucheron continued to make great use of the diamonds which had made the firm famous during the late nineteenth century, only now they were literally combined with lapis lazuli, jade, coral, onyx and other semi-precious stones; while the jewels of Lacloche Frères, Chaumet, Linzeler & Marshak, Dusausoy and so many other firms sparkled their way into the jewellery boxes and onto the necks, arms and clothes of the fashionable and rich men and women of the 1920s.

Elsewhere, the style was neither widespread nor much imitated, although occasional pieces were produced in Italy, Germany and Britain during the late 1920s. The Italian G Ravasco's diamond-studded geometric creations, or German jeweller Theodor Fahrner's later jewels, for example, were largely derivative of the noted French jewellers' designs, while Switzerland's expert watchmakers, many of whose designers were in any case often French, created cases with subtle geometric motifs.

## BRITISH JEWELLERS

Some London jewellers, like Asprey and Mappin & Webb, produced Art Deco-style confections, but these are largely unsigned, so the designers are unknown.

Some British designers, however, like Sybil Dunlop, Harold Stabler and H G Murphy, known primarily for their Arts and Crafts-style pieces, produced decidedly *moderne* (though not geometric) jewels. The Copenhagen firm of Georg Jensen, the Danish silversmith, produced silver jewellery in the Art Deco era (and some gold as well), adding sharp geometric forms to its repertoire of stylised motifs. Animal subjects – especially the perennially popular deer – as well as flowers and leaves, adorned brooches, bracelets and buckles, and these in turn were imitated by a host of European and American jewellers.

## AMERICAN JEWELLERY

American jewellery in the Art Deco period

was mostly designed in the French style by such fine firms as Tiffany & Co, Udall & Ballou, Spaulding-Gorham and C D Peacock. Bracelets, brooches and pendants were sometimes starkly geometric, but were far more often either simple floral arrangements or dazzling masses of coloured gems and diamonds. These included Oriental-inspired pieces, like a bracelet from Marsh & Co (a San Francisco jeweller), its carved coral plaques alternating with iron sections enclosing Chinese characters; architectonic confections, like a pair of gold Tiffany clips comprising stepped sections of tiny squares; and Egyptian-Revival baubles, such as Marcus & Co's opal brooch with an elaborate gold setting featuring a pharaoh and his queen, a scarab beetle and lotus flowers.

## THE AMERICAN STYLE

The indigenous Mexican silver industry was highlighted in the Art Deco era as a result of the talents of American architect-designer-teacher William Spratling, who settled in Taxco in 1929. He opened a shop dealing in traditional crafts and also started a school where he trained native people to work with silver and other local substances. Spratling produced some stunning brooches, bracelets and earrings, mostly in silver set with amethysts, but some of gold, all of which had a clean, crisp quality that was highly sympathetic to the native materials used. A whole community of jewellers sprang up in Taxco around Spratling and his wife.

Though French designs were often slightly toned down for wealthy, conservative clients, several significant jewellery manufacturers like New York's Oscar Heyman and Brothers, the

*Left: A design for a diamond and sapphire necklace, Oscar Heyman and Bros, c.1928.*

Bonner Manufacturing Company and Walter P McTeigue, Inc provided Saks Fifth Avenue and other exclusive department stores with their creations.

### THE *MODERNE* EMBRACED

Even the mail-order Sears, Roebuck catalogue featured *moderne* jewellery: diamond wedding rings in handsome geometric settings of platinum; bar pins and pendants featuring stepped designs; or watches boasting coloured-paste embellishments. Of course, there were also American jewellers akin to Cartier (which had a New York branch, as did Van Cleef & Arpels and others). Some of them even had designs made up in Paris for them. In the main, precious American Art Deco *bijoux* tend to be more colourful than their Gallic counterparts.

### THE DECLINE OF LUXURY

From 1930 the effects of the Depression were felt in luxury items. After the crash of 1929, and as the economic effects of the Depression deepened, firms were hesitant to produce new items which might prove difficult to sell.

Indeed, the 1925 Exposition had been the high point in Art Deco jewellery, accessories and *objets d'art*. After this date, forms grew larger and more massive. Colour was toned down until black and white predominated. The

*Left: Cartier created this onyx and pavé-set diamond pendant brooch with its pearl-scattered, detachable tassel. It represents quintessentially* moderne *jewel.*

*Below: This 1930s' Tiffany & Co brooch in the unlikely guise of a swordfish is made up of diamonds, emeralds, sapphires and a ruby.*

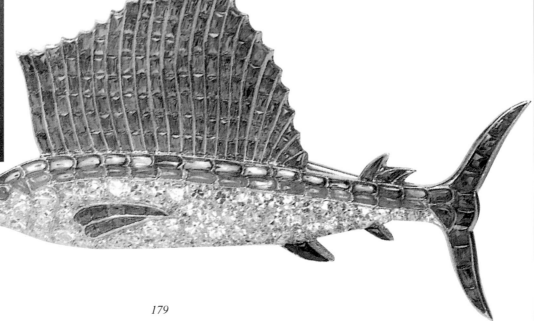

spirit of the period gradually faded and, with the advent of the Depression, the demand for luxury goods was severely reduced. The major jewellery houses cut back their staff or closed.

In 1935, Art Deco's grand master Georges Fouquet ceased major production. In the United States, Tiffany's remained open but operated with no additional staff. By this time the influence of the Bauhaus had been felt in all phases and spheres of the decorative arts. Industrial design, which was based on machine production, was assimilated into a design paradigm for the masses. The spirit of Art Deco had waned.

### CHEAPER ALTERNATIVES
Geometric rings, clips, brooches, bracelets, lapel watches and necklaces abounded, made from precious metals and jewels as well as of base metals or new alloys, paste, marcasite, plastic and stones such as dark-red carnelian and apple-green chrysoprase – both chalcedonies and cheaper to use than the coral and jade that they resembled. Indeed, during the 1920s, the introduction of synthetic substances brought the price of artificial jewellery within the reach of the general population, and the Art Deco period therefore also spawned thousands of cheap, anonymous designs, many of which are now highly sought after by collectors today.

### NEW MATERIALS
Art Deco costume jewellery, which was made out of base metals or silver set with marcasite, paste or imitation stones, included bracelets, brooches, barrettes and clips – for ears, shoes, lapels – in coloured Bakelite, Celluloid, galalite and other synthetics, often in geometric shapes

*Right: This French necklace, made of silver, paste and jade, dates from the mid-1920s.*

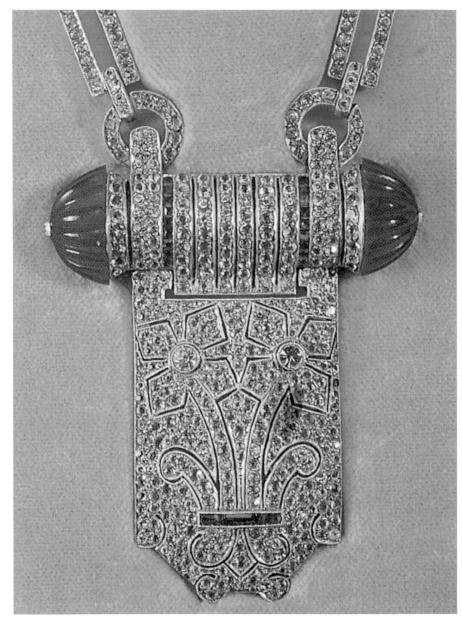

or carved as stylised flowers.

## COSTUME JEWELLERY

During the 1920s and 1930s, costume jewellery, especially with the imprimaturs of the trendsetting couturiers Coco Chanel – who championed the use of costume jewellery from the early 1920s – and Elsa Schiaparelli became ever more popular, outrageous and yet acceptable – from garish paste chokers and earrings to comical plastic-fish bangles, and (from Schiaparelli) a coloured-metal, zodiac-sign necklace. Chanel especially utilised carved beads in her designs for imitation jewellery. Czechoslovakia, long a producer of glass beads, made inexpensive necklaces, pins and other bits of jewellery which were sometimes quite striking, with strong angles and colours.

## AMUSING MOTIFS

The motifs of Art Deco costume jewels range from the sublime to the ridiculous: from stunning geometric configurations of paste to silly plastic cherries dangling from a wooden bar. The former borrowed its subject from *deluxe* jewellery of the time, but the latter – a joke – came about more or less on its own.

## FIGURAL SUBJECTS

Unlike much of the jewellery in preceding eras, animals and people inhabited the world of 1920s' and 1930s' costume jewellery, from gentle silver fawns and playful plastic Scotty dogs to paste, turquoise and marcasite Chinese men and elegant gilt-metal, cloche-hatted vamps. Flowers in every possible colour, combination and variety sprouted on gilt-metal or

*Left: This attractive set includes ear-clips, a necklace and an expandable bracelet of gilt metal and casein, a type of plastic.*

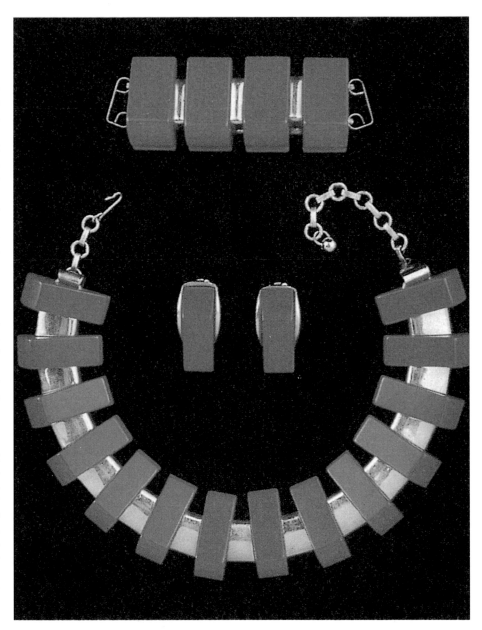

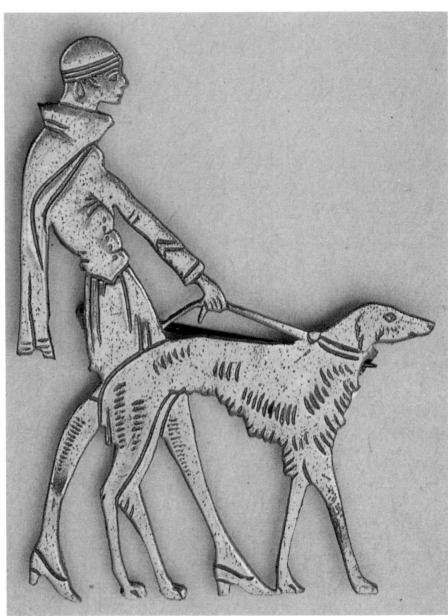

*Above: This 1930s' silver deer pin is set with marcasites grouped to form patterns.*

*Left: An elegant lady walking her dog is the subject of this yellow-metal 1930s' brooch.*

silver brooches and pendants, their paste petals glittering shamelessly.

During the late 1930s, however, sophisticated yet free-form designs began to appear (in both fine and costume jewellery, but especially the latter), with ribbons, bows, loops and scrolls the predominant decorative motifs. The Napier and Coro companies in the USA were at the forefront of the manufacture of these so-called 'cocktail jewels', which were highly kinetic and full of energy, unlike the more serene, decorative pieces of a decade or so earlier.

### COSTUME JEWELLERY REAPPRAISED

Art Deco costume jewellery – lovely, imaginative, fun or all three – has surely come into its own in recent years. In its own time, the

*Below: This aeroplane pin commemorates Charles Lindbergh's transatlantic flight.*

NEW YORK TO PARIS
MAY 21, 1927

KING OF THE AIR

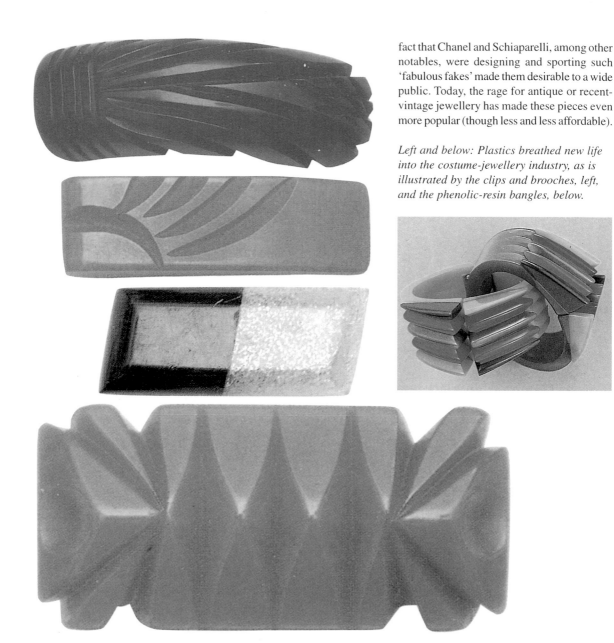

fact that Chanel and Schiaparelli, among other notables, were designing and sporting such 'fabulous fakes' made them desirable to a wide public. Today, the rage for antique or recent-vintage jewellery has made these pieces even more popular (though less and less affordable).

*Left and below: Plastics breathed new life into the costume-jewellery industry, as is illustrated by the clips and brooches, left, and the phenolic-resin bangles, below.*

# USEFUL INFORMATION

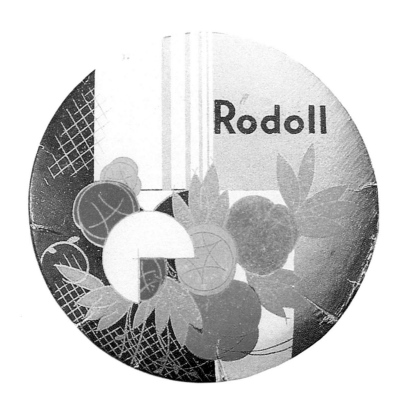

# MUSEUMS WITH ART DECO COLLECTIONS

Most Art Deco items are in private or company collections. Furthermore, few art museums have special Art Deco collections, though many host travelling Art Deco exhibitions from time to time. Here are a few museums that have Art Deco items of particular interest.

AUSTRIA
Historical Museum of the City of Vienna
Karlsplatz
1040 Vienna 4

Museum of the 20th Century
Schweizergarten
1030 Vienna 3

CZECH REPUBLIC
Arts and Crafts Museum
Stare Mesto 17
Listopodu 2, Prague

CANADA
Art Gallery of Ontario
317 Dundas Street West
Toronto
Ontario

UNITED KINGDOM
Brighton Museum
The Old Steyne
Brighton, West Sussex

Victoria and Albert Museum
Exhibition Road
London SW7

Gerald Wells Radio Collection
23 Rosendale Road
Dulwich
London SE21

Jeffrye Museum
London E2

Southend Museum
Southend, Essex

York Castle Museum
York, Yorkshire

Lakeland Motor Museum
Export Centre
New Road
Blackpool, Lancashire

FRANCE
Musée des Arts Décoratifs
107-109 rue de Rivoli
Paris 1

Musée de l'Ecole de Nancy
38 rue du Sergent-Blandan
Nancy

Musée de la Publicité
rue du Paradis
Paris, 10e

DENMARK
Museum of Decorative Art
Copenhagen

*Previous page: A simple floral motif on a French powder box.*

GERMANY
Ursula and Hans Kolsch
AM Ruhrstein 37B
D-43 Essen 1

SWEDEN
Nordiska Museet
Stockholm

Rohsska Konstslo jdmuseet
Gothenburg

UNITED STATES OF AMERICA
Drexel Museum
Drexel University
Drexel
Pennsylvania 19104

University of Washington Costume and
Textile Study Center
Seattle
Washington 98105

Baker Furniture Museum
Holland
Michigan 49423

R.M.S. Queen Mary
Long Beach
California 90803

Norton Simon Museum of Art
Pasadena
California 91101

Barnsdall House Museum
Los Angeles
California 90029
(building designed by Frank Lloyd Wright)

Art Institute of Chicago
Michigan Avenue
Chicago, Illinois

Museum of Contemporary Art
Ontario Street
Chicago
Illinois 60611

National Museum of American Art
Smithsonian Institute
Washington D.C.

Goodyear Rubber Exhibit
1144 E. Market Street
Akron
Ohio 44316

Metropolitan Museum of Art
5th Avenue and West 82nd Street
New York City
New York 10028

Cooper Hewitt Museum of Decorative Arts
2 East 91st Street
New York City
New York 10028

Solomon R. Guggenheim Museum
1071 5th Avenue
New York City
New York 10028
(building designed by Frank Lloyd Wright)

# FURTHER READING

Adam, P, *Eileen Grey*
Thames and Hudson, London, 1987.

Banham, R, *Theory and Design in the First Machine Age*
London, 1960.

Barnicoat, M, *Posters: A Concise History*
Thames and Hudson, London, 1988.

Battersby, M, *The Decorative Twenties*
Studio Vista, London, 1971.

Bel Geddes, N, *Horizons*
Dover Books, New York, 1977.

Bernstein, M A, *The Great Depression*
Cambridge Press, New York, 1987.

Brinnin, J M & Gaulin, K, *Grand Luxe, The Transatlantic Style*
Bloomsbury, London, 1988.

Burness, T, *Cars of the Early Thirties*
Chilton, London, 1970.

Camard, F, *Ruhlmann, Master of Art Deco*
Thames and Hudson, London, 1984.

Foucart, B; Offrey, C; Rubichon, F; Villers, C, *Normandie*
Thames and Hudson, London, 1986.

Gallo, M, *The Poster in History*
Hamlyn, London, 1974.

Goldberger, P, *The Skyscraper*
Allen Lane, London, 1982.

Hannah, F, *Ceramics*
Bell and Hyman, London, 1976.

Heskett, J, *Industrial Design*
Thames and Hudson, London, 1980.

Levey, M, *London Transport Posters*
Phaidon, London, 1976.

Lynam, R, *Paris Fashion*
Michael Joseph, London, 1972.

MacGowan, K, *Behind the Screen*
Delacorte Press, New York, 1965.

Meadmore, C, *The Modern Chair*
Van Nostrand Rheinhold Company, London, 1979.

Meikle, J L, *Twentieth Century Limited*; *Industrial Design in America 1925-39*
Temple University Press, Philadelphia, 1979.

Mouron, H, *Cassandre*
Thames and Hudson, London, 1985.

Nobbs, G, *The Wireless Stars*
Wensum Books, Norwich, 1972.

Pawley, E, *BBC Engineering 1922-72*
BBC Books, London, 1972.

Pevsner, N, *Pioneers of Modern Design*
Harmondsworth, London 1960.

Phillips, L (ed), *High Style*; *20th Century American Design*
Summit Books, Whitney Museum of American Art, New York, 1985.

Raulet, S, *Art Deco Jewellery*
Thames and Hudson, London, 1985.

Whitfort, F, *Bauhaus*
Thames and Hudson, London, 1984.

Whittick, A, *European Architecture in the 20th Century*
Leonard Hill, England, 1972.

Wilson, R G, *The Machine Age in America*
Metropolitan Museum of Art, New York, 1986.

# ACKNOWLEDGEMENTS

The material in this book previously appeared in:

*Art Deco Painting and Design*
*Art Deco Furniture and Metalwork*
*Art Deco Fashion and Jewellery*
*Art Deco Source Book,*
*Art Deco: An Illustrated Guide to the Decorative Style 1920–40*
*20s and 30s Style*


Quantum Publishing would like to thank Rod Teasdale for jacket design.